In Praise of Philosophy and Other Essays

T0325242

In Praise of Philosophy and Other Essays

Maurice Merleau-Ponty

Translated by
JOHN WILD AND JAMES EDIE
JOHN O'NEILL

NORTHWESTERN UNIVERSITY PRESS

Contents

In Praise of Philosophy

Translated by John Wild and James Edie

In Praise of Philosophy

Mister Provost, Colleagues, Ladies and Gentlemen:

The man who witnesses his own research, that
is to say his own inner disorder, cannot feel himself to be the heir of the distinguished men whose
names he sees on these walls.[1] If, in addition, he is
a philosopher, that is to say if he knows that he
knows nothing, how could he believe himself justified in occupying this chair, and how could he even
desire to do so? The answer to these questions is
very simple. Since its foundation the Collège de
France has been charged with the duty, not of giving
to its hearers already-acquired truths, but the idea
of free investigation. If, last winter, the Collège de
France desired to maintain a chair of philosophy,
it is because philosophical ignorance puts the crown-

1. This is the text of the inaugural lecture. Some notes which
were not read have been placed at the end of the volume

ing touch on the spirit of search to which it is devoted. If a philosopher solicits your votes, my dear
colleagues, it is, you well know, in order to live the
philosophical life more completely. And if you have
elected him, it is to support this endeavor in his person. Although I feel unequal to the honor, I am
nevertheless happy to undertake the task, since it is
a great good fortune, as Stendhal said, for one "to
have his passion as a profession." I have been
touched at finding you so resolved, all other considerations aside, in desiring to maintain philosophy
in your midst, and it is a pleasure to thank you for
this today.

Without doubt I could not do better than to examine before you the function of the philosopher,
first of all as it was exercised by my predecessors,
and then as it pertains to this function to consider
both the past of philosophy and its present.

I / Lavelle[2]

THE PHILOSOPHER IS MARKED by the distinguish-
ing trait that he possesses *inseparably* the taste
for evidence and the feeling for ambiguity. When
he limits himself to accepting ambiguity, it is

2. For purposes of clarification the translators have added
titles to the various sections of this lecture, and certain long
paragraphs have been divided.

called equivocation. But among the great it becomes a theme; it contributes to establishing certitudes rather than menacing them. Therefore it is necessary to distinguish good and bad ambiguity. Even those who have desired to work out a completely positive philosophy have been philosophers only to the extent that, at the same time, they have refused the right to install themselves in absolute knowledge. They taught not this knowledge, but its becoming in us, not the absolute but, at most, our *absolute relation* to it, as Kierkegaard said. What makes a philosopher is the movement which leads back without ceasing from knowledge to ignorance, from ignorance to knowledge, and a kind of rest in this movement.

Even conceptions as limpid as those which M. Lavelle so deliberately oriented toward pure being would verify this definition of the philosopher. Lavelle gave as the object of philosophy "this whole of being in which our own existence is being inscribed by a continuous miracle." He spoke of a miracle because there is a paradox here: the paradox of a total being which is, in advance, everything which we can be and do, and yet which would not be it without us, and which thus needs to be augmented by our own being. Our relation with being involves a double sense, the first according to which we belong to it, the second according to which it belongs to us. We cannot, therefore, place ourselves in

being in order to derive ourselves and the world
from it. If we do this, it is only possible, says Lavelle, "by dissimulating that both are already
known." My situation in the world before any reflexion, and my initiation into existence cannot be
reabsorbed by the reflexion which goes beyond
them towards the absolute, nor can they be treated
afterwards as effects. The movement by which we
go from ourselves towards the absolute continually
underlies the descending movement which detached thought accomplishes by going from the absolute towards itself. In fact, what the philosopher
poses is never absolutely absolute; it is the absolute
with respect to him. With these ideas of participation and presence, Lavelle rightly tried to define a
relationship between ourselves and total being
which always remains reciprocal to some extent.

His works thus had to develop on two sides. First
of all, the world, that profound treasure in which the
naive man thinks he discovers the primordial meaning of being, appears to Lavelle without depth and
without mystery. It is the *phenomenon,* that which
appears and has no interior. We could not have
learned the meaning of the word "being" merely
by considering this scenery. It is in ourselves and
only in ourselves that we can touch the interior of
being, because it is only there that we discover a
being which has an interior and which is nothing

but this interior. There is thus no transitive relation between me and my body, me and the world, and it is only "towards the within" that the self can overflow. My only commerce is with a perfect interiority, the model (but also, we shall see, the copy) of the imperfect interiority which defines me. Meditation on being is localized in the *self* and in *the more myself than myself*, behind the world and history. From this point of view philosophy has scarcely any problems or anything to do. Its sole task is to remind men of a participation in universal being which they could never completely forget without ceasing to be, and which, in the words of the preface to *Présence totale*, has always been entrusted to the *philosophia perennis*. Hence the philosopher has nothing to do in history, or in the debates of his period. Prefacing a book of political philosophy, Lavelle wrote that spiritual reform will reform the state "without anyone having had to think about it."

Then there is the other side. An infinite ego is not an *I*. For Lavelle only a being who suffers can say *I*. Thus I do not have a true knowledge of God through myself. It is only by carrying himself beyond himself, by faith, that the philosopher can pose God, says Lavelle, and for this very reason he can never think from the point of view of God. There is a truth of the world and of thought according to the world. For it, God is "the infinite Solitary, the perfectly Separated, the eternally Absent," says Lavelle. And it is because God is inaccessible to us, and without ever ceasing to be inaccessible, that he becomes present to our own solitude and our own separation. Thus our relation to being, which was thought to be entirely positive, is now hollowed out with a double negation. And the result is that, in order to pose itself, this relation has need of the world which but a minute ago was only an appearance. The visible evidence of interiority now reassumes its importance; it is not a borrowed garment but the incarnation of interiority. Thought without language, says Lavelle, would not be a purer thought; it would be no more than the intention to think. And his last book offers a theory of expressiveness which makes of expression not "a faithful image of an already realized interior being, but the very means by which it is realized." The sensible and the phenomenon, he continues, not only limit our participation in being; "we incorporate them into the positive essence of each being in such a way that we can say, if not that being is only what appears, it is at least that by which it appears." Here there is no longer any alternative between the phenomenon, or matter, and being, or the spirit. True spiritualism, writes Lavelle, consists in rejecting the alternatives of spiritualism and materialism. Philosophy thus cannot consist in turning our attention from matter to the spirit or complete itself in the non-temporal affirmation of a non-temporal interiority. There is, says Lavelle, only "the philosophy of to-day, that which I can think and live now." [3]

At the bottom of Lavelle's thought, perhaps, lay the idea that the unfolding of time and the world is the same thing as their consummation in the past. But this also means that one does not go beyond the world except by entering into it and that the spirit makes use of the world, time, speech, and history in a single movement and animates them with a meaning which is never used up. It would be the function of philosophy, then, to record this passage of meaning rather than to take it as an accomplished fact. Lavelle never says this. But it seems to us that his idea of a central function of the temporal present turned him away from a retrospective philosophy which would convert the world and history into a universal past in advance.

II / Bergson

IT IS IN THIS POINT of the present that Lavelle's descending dialectic crossed the ascending dialectic of Bergson and Le Roy. We name them together in spite of the differences which we will emphasize later, because their ideas should no more be separated in what we say of them than they were meant to be in their development. Bergson and Le

3. See Note I at the end of the volume.

Roy began from the world and constituted time. But they arrived at what inwardly animates world and time, at what Bergson called the *hesitation of time* and what Le Roy called *invention*. They reached, on its temporal side, the same joining of happening and meaning which preoccupied the later Lavelle, and we find at this point in their research the same ambiguous sparkle.

What we are saying here is discovered only after one has gone beyond the first appearance of Bergsonism. For there is even in Bergson a completely positive way of presenting the intuition of the *durée*, of matter, of life, and of God. Is not the discovery of the *durée* at first the discovery of a second reality in which the instant at the very moment of its passage maintains itself, conserves itself undivided in the present, and grows? Is not the *durée* a kind of flowing thing which remains while it melts away? And do not the later studies of Bergson consist in rediscovering in *other things*, in matter, in life, the same real cohesion at first disclosed in us? The last pages of *Matter and Memory* speak of a "presentiment" and of an "imitation" of memory in matter. *Creative Evolution* attaches life, in the terms of Bergson, "either to consciousness itself, or to something that resembles it." And how could something resemble consciousness if the consciousness we are thinking of does not already have the fullness of a thing? At times Bergson treats of consciousness as a substance spread out through the universe, which in rudimentary organisms is "compressed in a kind of vise" and which in those more differentiated organisms is allowed to develop. What then is this "large current of consciousness," without organism, without individuality, which Bergson says runs through matter? Viewed as a cosmological factor, consciousness is unrecognizable. When Bergson later on expressly identifies it with God, it is difficult to recognize an ego in this "center from which all worlds spring forth like the stems of an immense bouquet." It is the God of mystical experience who in the *Two Sources* definitively gives personality to cosmological consciousness. But even then the Bergsonian God remains very different from anything we can call thought or will because it excludes the negative component. Divine thought or will, says Bergson, is "too full of itself" for us to find in it the idea of nonbeing. "This would be a weakness incompatible with its nature, which is force." Held between the two Powers, God, who is force, and life, which is action, man, as he is, can only appear as a failure. He is the phantom of a "divine humanity" which, says Bergson, "should have existed theoretically from the beginning," and history, the communicative life of men, is not an autonomous order. It oscillates between the frenzy of action and mysticism; it is not in this history that we will find the guiding thread.

Fullness of the *durée*, primordial fullness of

cosmological consciousness, fullness of God, these results imply a theory of intuition as coincidence or
contact. And in fact Bergson defined philosophy as a
"semi-divine" state in which all the problems which
"put us in the presence of emptiness" are ignored.
Why have I been born? Why is there something
rather than nothing? How can I know anything?
These traditional questions are "pathological" for
Bergson, like those of the doubter who no longer
knows whether he has closed the window. They only
appear when we try to place ourselves intellectually
in a primordial emptiness, whereas emptiness, non-
being, nothingness, disorder are never anything
other than a purely verbal way of saying that we expected something else, and thus they presuppose a
subject already installed in being. Philosophy, true
thought, which is entirely positive, will rediscover
this naive contact already presupposed in the apparatus of negation and language in general. This
true thought Bergson frequently calls "fusion" with
things or "inscription," "recording," "impression" of
things in us. It seeks less to "resolve" classical problems than to "dissolve" them. "Simple act," "viewing
without a point of view," direct access without interposed symbols to the interior of things—all these
celebrated formulas of intuition define it as a massive grip on being, without exploration, without interior movement of meaning.

This is an aspect of Bergsonism which is the easiest to see. But it is not the only one, nor the most valid. For these formulas express less what Bergson had to say than his break with received doctrine at the time he began his research. It is said that he restored intuition against the intellect and logic, spirit against matter, life against mechanism. This is how both his friends and his adversaries understood him when his studies appeared. But his adversaries have missed the point. Perhaps it is time to look in Bergson for something more than the antithesis to their abandoned theses. In spite of the paradox, the wholly positive Bergson is a polemic writer, and as the negative begins to reappear in his philosophy, it is progressively affirmed. It would perhaps show more attention to his writings if we were to look in them for his views on the living and difficult relations of the spirit with the body and the world, rather than for the critique of Taine and Spencer; to look for the interior movement which animates his intuitions, which ties them to one another, and which frequently reverses their initial relationships, rather than for successive assertions. In this way Bergson would be truly delivered from his adversaries, delivered also from his "friends" who, as Péguy has already said, understood him no better. And we would recognize at the same time the soundness of studies like those of Le Roy, which never stop at Bergsonian positivism but which, on essential points like the theory of intuition and of the immediate and the limit, give Bergsonism its most authentic interpretation.

Bergson wanted to be finished with traditional problems, not to eliminate the problematic of philosophy but to revivify it. He saw so clearly that all philosophy must be, in the words of Le Roy, a new philosophy, that it is so little the discovery of a solution inscribed in being which satisfies our curiosity, that he demands of it not only the invention of solutions but the invention of its own problems. In 1935 he wrote: "I call an *amateur* in philosophy anyone who accepts the terms of a usual problem as they are . . . doing philosophy authentically would consist in *creating* the framework of the problem and of *creating* the solution." Thus when he says that well-posed problems are very close to being solved, this does not mean that we have already *found* what we are looking for, but that we have already invented it. It is not that there would be a question in us and a response in things, an exterior being to be discovered by an observing consciousness; the solution is also in us, and being itself is problematic. Something of the nature of the question passes into the answer.

The famous Bergsonian coincidence certainly does not mean, then, that the philosopher loses himself or is absorbed into being. We must say rather that he experiences himself as transcended by being. It is not necessary for him to go outside himself in order to reach the things themselves; he is solicited or haunted by them from within. For an ego which is *durée* cannot grasp another being except in the form of another *durée*. By experiencing my own manner of using up time, I grasp it, says Bergson, as a "choice among an infinity of possible *durées*." There is a "singular nature" of the *durée* which makes it at once my manner of being and a universal dimension for other beings in such a way that what is "superior" and "inferior" to us still remains "in a certain sense, interior to us." What I observe is a concordance and a discordance of things with my *durée;* these are the things with me in a lateral relationship of coexistence. I have the idea of a *durée* of the universe distinct from mine only because it extends the whole length of mine and because it is necessary that something in the melting sugar respond to my waiting for a glass of sugar water. When we are at the source of the *durée,* we are also at the heart of things because they are the adversity which makes us wait. The relation of the philosopher to being is not the frontal relation of the spectator to the spectacle; it is a kind of complicity, an oblique and clandestine relationship. We understand now how Bergson can say that the absolute is "very close to us and, in a certain measure, in us." It is in the way in which things modulate our *durée*.

If to do philosophy is to discover the primary sense of being, then one does not philosophize in quitting the human situation; it is necessary rather to plunge into it. The absolute knowledge of the philosopher is perception. "Suppose," says the first Oxford Conference, "that instead of wishing to elevate ourselves above our perception of things, we immerse ourselves in it in order to bore into this perception and enlarge it . . . , we would have a philosophy to which it would be impossible to oppose others, because it would not have left anything outside itself which other doctrines could pick up; it would have taken everything." Perception grounds everything because it shows us, so to speak, an obsessional relation with being; it is there before us, and yet it touches us from within. "Whatever the intimate essence of that which is and of that which happens may be," says Bergson, "we are of it." Perhaps he did not understand the full meaning of these words. We can see here an allusion to an objective evolution which brings man out of animality, the animal from cosmological consciousness, cosmological consciousness from God, and which would have left some sediments in us. Philosophy would in that case consist in dating these sediments. It would be a cosmological construction. Consciousness would look for its ancestors in things; it would project into them souls or analogues of souls; philosophy would be a panpsychism. But, since Bergson says that it is a generalized perception, it is in actual and present perception, not in some now completed genesis, that it is necessary to search for the relationship of our being with things.

"We are of it" thus means that these colors, these objects which we see, decorate and inhabit even our dreams, that these animals are humorous variants of ourselves, that all beings are symbolic of our life, and that this is what we see in them. Matter, life, God are not "interior" to us, as Bergson says, if by "matter" we mean the matter in itself which appeared one day through a kind of failing of the transcendent principle; if by "life" we mean life in itself, that feeble movement which once upon a time palpitated in a little newly made protoplasm; if by "God" we mean God in himself, the "immense" force which hangs over us. It can only be a question of matter, of life, of God in so far as they are perceived by us. The genesis which the works of Bergson trace is a history of ourselves which we tell to ourselves; it is a natural myth by which we express our ability to get along with all the forms of being. We are not this pebble, but when we look at it, it awakens resonances in our perceptive apparatus; our perception appears to come from it. That is to say our perception of the pebble is a kind of promotion to (conscious) existence for itself; it is our recovery of this mute thing which, from the time it enters our life, begins to unfold its implicit being, which is revealed to itself through us. What we believed to be coincidence is coexistence.

Perhaps Bergson began by understanding philosophy as a simple return to what is *given,* but later on he saw that this secondary, laborious, rediscovered naiveté does not merge us with a previous reality, does not identify us with the thing itself, without any point of view, without symbol, without perspective. Formulas like "sounding," "auscultation," "palpation," which are better, make it sufficiently clear that intuition needs to be understood, that it is necessary for me to appropriate to myself a meaning in it which is still captive. What precisely is intuitive in intuition? Bergson admits that most of the time it is present to the philosopher only in the form of a certain "power of negation" that excludes theses which are insufficient. Should we suppose a positive and already made view which underlies these negative appearances and sustains them? This would be to give way to the retrospective illusion, precisely criticized by Bergson. The global view which he calls intuition orients the whole effort of expression of the philosopher, but it does not contain it in abridged form. We would be wrong in imagining in Berkeley, before he thought or wrote, an abridged Berkeley which would have contained his whole philosophy and more. We would be wrong in believing, though Bergson said so, that the philosopher speaks all his life *for want of* being able to say this "infinitely simple thing" forever concentrated "in a single point" of himself. He also speaks *to say it,* because it demands to be said, because it is not achieved before it has been said. It is perfectly true that each philosopher, each painter, considers what the others call his work as the simple rough sketch of a work which still remains to be done. This does not prove that this work exists somewhere within themselves and they have only to lift a veil to reach it.

M. Gueroult showed in this very place last year that the secret and the center of a philosophy does not lie in a prenatal inspiration, but that it develops as the work progresses, that it is a becoming-meaning, which builds itself in accord with itself and in reaction against itself, that a philosophy is necessarily a (philosophical) history, an exchange between problems and solutions in which each partial solution transforms the initial problem in such wise that the meaning of the whole does not pre-exist it, except as a style pre-exists its works, and seems, after the fact, to announce them. What Gueroult says here of intuition applied to philosophical systems, we can say in general of philosophical intuition, and this time with Bergson's consent. It is proper to intuition to call forth a development, to become what it is, because it contains a double reference to the mute being which it interrogates, and to the tractable [*maniable*] meaning which is derived from it. It is the experience of their concordance; it is, as Bergson happily said, a *reading*, the art of grasping a meaning in a style before it has been put into concepts. And finally *the thing itself* is the virtual focal point of these convergent formulations.

The more energetic our intention to see the things themselves, the more the appearances by which they are expressed and the words by which we express them will be interposed between these things and us. In the very measure to which Bergson succeeded in showing that emptiness, nothingness, or disorder is never in things, that there are, outside of us, only presences, he came to designate ubiquity as the fundamental property of our spirit, the power of being elsewhere and of aiming at being only indirectly and obliquely. He says very well that the spirit "refuses to keep its place and concentrates all its attention on this refusal; it never determines its actual position except with respect to the one it has just left, like a passenger at the rear of a train who sees only the places he has left behind." Are we not always in the position of this traveler? Are we ever at the point of objective space which our body occupies? Is not our insertion in space always indirect, reflected towards us by the perspectival aspect of things which indicates the location which *should* be ours? In order to be able to treat this indirect relation and this distance with respect to being as a bad habit of the practical intellect, it is necessary to expel non-being from the world and, then, from ourselves.

Bergson thought he had done this by showing

that a nothingness in consciousness would be the consciousness of a nothingness, and that it would, therefore, not be nothing. But this is to say in other words that the being of consciousness is made of a substance so subtle that it is not less consciousness in the consciousness of an emptiness than in that of a thing. The primary being with respect to nothingness is thus not the natural or positive being of things; it is, Bergson himself says, existence in a Kantian sense, radical contingency. And if true philosophy dispels the vertigo and the anxiety that come from the idea of nothingness, it is because it interiorizes them, because it incorporates them into being and conserves them in the vibration of the being which is becoming. "If we refuse the intuition of emptiness," wrote M. Bachelard, "we have the right to refuse the intuition of fullness . . . This is as much as to say that, after various transpositions, we find the fundamental dialectic of being and nothingness stretched out in time. We thus give Bergson's formula its full ontological and temporal meaning: time is hesitation."

Le Roy turned Bergsonism away from a massive realism a long time ago. For him intuition is a "colored moment of the *cogito,*" that is to say, a *cogito* which does not only render me certain, in the restrictive sense, of *my* thought, but also of what responds to it in the singular aspect of each thing. It is the experience of a thought which is sleeping in things and which is awakened at the approach of my thought. For Le Roy the famous "images" of the first chapter of *Matter and Memory* become, in his own words, "the lightning-flash of existence," the point at which I make the real "gleam" and reveal itself. Immediate experience is what awakens in me this fundamental phenomenon and what changes the "wholeness of its object into a group of living operations." When known being coincides with being, it is not because it fuses with it. Being is for the intuition a limit in the true sense of the word, that is to say, according to Le Roy, "a certain style of movement immanent in the very succession of stages, a certain quality of progression discernible by intrinsic comparisons," a "converging character" of the series. Thus Le Roy gave intuition a component of negativity and ambiguity without which it would be blind.

To get a true idea of Bergsonism it would now be necessary to take up his fundamental intuitions one by one and show how the initial positivism is transcended in each of them. Jean Hyppolite has recently begun this work in so far as it concerns the intuition of the *durée*. He has shown that the *durée* of the *Essay on the Immediate Data of Consciousness*, the undividedness of the interior life which is preserved whole, becomes, in *Matter and Memory*, a system of oppositions between the emptiness of the past, the emptiness of the future, and the fullness of the present, like the oppositions between time and space. The very nature of the *durée* now requires that it be internally divided into these three dimensions and that it receive in itself the body and spatiality which constitute the present and without which even the past would remain nebulous and would not be evoked, that is to say recovered and expressed. Henceforth the spirit is no longer undividedness; it is what "strives to gather itself together," as Hyppolite says, between the two limits of pure memory and pure action, which are synonyms of unconsciousness.[4]

One could note an analogous movement in the intuition of life. There are moments in which it is no longer the fusion of the philosopher with a consciousness in things, but the consciousness of an agreement between itself and the phenomena. Then it is no longer a question of explaining life but of deciphering it, says Bergson, as a painter deciphers a face. It is necessary to rediscover "the intention of life, the simple movement which runs through the lines, which ties them to one another and gives them a meaning." We are capable of this kind of reading because we carry in our incarnate being the alphabet and the grammar of life, but this does not presuppose an achieved meaning either in us or in it.[5] Here again Le Roy resolutely followed the better direction of Bergsonism when he defined life as a

4. See Note II at the end of the volume.
5. See Note III at the end of the volume.

"groping finality," in which end and means, meaning and chance call forth one another. We do not recognize in this pregnant finality, in this meaning in labor, the sovereign ease of the cosmological consciousness which lets fall out of itself, with a simple gesture, like a movement of our hand, all the details that constitute the life of an organism.

For even greater reason it is necessary to ask if the intuition of God in Bergson is summed up in the God "who is force," of which we have spoken above. We know that he briefly defined the being of God as a *durée* that is more *durée* than our own. It is, he says, the "concentration" of every *durée*, and he calls it the "eternity of life," which *eminently* contains our *durée*. But this is to say that, in going from God to us, we go from the greater to the lesser, and that this lesser does not need explanation, since nothingness, as Malebranche said, has no properties. But we have just seen Bergson ultimately define our *durée* by the double nothingness which the future and the past oppose to the present, by a break in the fullness of being. If God is truly eternity of life, if, as Bergson says, "he is not at all fully realized," it is necessary that negativity penetrate the God "who is force." Is it enough to say here what Bergson puts in the mouth of Ravaisson, that "infinite Thought has annulled something of the plenitude of its being in order to take from it, by a kind of awakening and resurrection, everything which exists"? But if God really broke himself open in order to install the negative within himself, and if beings only appear in the opposite movement of change, they do not proceed from him. He is not a principle from which we can descend towards our *durée* and the world; he is a God towards whom we climb, whom the *durée* divines at each moment of its growth—as we sense an imminent phantasm at the edge of our visual field— but which cannot be *fixed*, cannot be known, and which cannot be independent of it and for itself.

This is even more striking in what Bergson says of God as the principle of the good. We know that he energetically rejected the arguments of classical theodicy which make evil a lesser good. "The philosopher," he says, "can content himself with arguments of this kind in the silence of his office. What will he think of them before a mother who has just seen her child die?" The only optimism he admits is an "empirical" optimism: the fact is that men, in spite of everything, accept life, and also there is a joy beyond pleasure and pain. This optimism does not *justify* suffering by joy, as its condition. It presupposes nothing like an infinite regard which, penetrating the world and the obscurity of suffering through and through, would be the equivalent of an approbation. Everything happens, according to Bergson, as if man encountered at the roots of his constituted being a generosity which is not a compromise with the adversity of the world and which is on his side against it. In rejecting the idea of God as a theoretical explanation, Le Roy says the same thing more energetically: ". . . We know God by his very life in us, in the work of our deification. In this sense we can even say that, for us, God is not, but that he is becoming." There is in Bergsonian theology, as perhaps in every theology since Christianity, an ambiguity thanks to which we never know if it is God who sustains men in their human being or if it is the inverse, since in order to know his existence it is necessary to pass through ours, and this is not an optional detour.

With respect to God who is force, our existence was a failure and the world a decadence which we could not heal except by returning here below. To the God who is on the side of men corresponds, on the contrary, a forward-looking history which is an experience searching for its accomplishment. Bergson's critique of the idea of progress aims at a progress without contingency, which would happen of itself. That is a particular case of the retrospective illusion. We see in a happening of the past the preparation of our present, whereas this past was "a complete act" in its time and it is the present success which transforms it into a rough design. But this underlines precisely the strange power we have of reviving the past, of inventing a sequel for it. Even if there is a metamorphosis here, it would not take place without a common meaning of the past and of the present. Bergson thus admits a sense of history as it develops and a progress, on condition that this is not a force which would act of itself, but which would be understood as something more to be made than observed, defined not by an *idea* but by a constant *orientation*. Granted this, there is nothing in history that is completely without meaning. Its dichotomies, its impasses, its returnings to abandoned paths, its discords have the appearance of non-sense only for an abstract mind which would reduce the problems of history to the problems of ideas.

But it is not merely a question here of confronting ideas but of incarnating them and of making them live, and in this respect we cannot know what they are capable of except by trying them out. This attempt involves a taking of sides and a struggle. The struggle here, says Bergson, is thus only "the superficial aspect of progress." It is well that the primordial unity was broken in order that the world and history might take place. The discord of man with himself, which up to now impeded him from being the "divine man," now constitutes his reality and his value. He is divided because he is not a "species" or a "created thing," because he is a "creative effort." He is a "realized contradiction," Bergson says, because humanity cannot validly "constitute itself ultimately without the aid of man himself." The undividedness of the origins is a symbol which our present will to be gives as both body and mind. It is the invitation to create out of nothing a body of institutions in which the spirit can recognize itself. Hence Bergson's unconservative tone, whether it is a question of machinism, leisure for the working-man, or the status of women. On this point also Le Roy anticipated the latent sense of Bergsonism when he spoke of our whole history as a revolution that has been developing since the Renaissance and when he spoke of the "absolute value of humanization" [*hominisation*].

We can summarize the internal movement of Bergsonism by saying that it is the development from a philosophy of impression to a philosophy of expression. What Bergson said against language has caused us to forget what he said in its favor. There is the language frozen on paper or in discontinuous elements in space, and there is the living word, the equal and the rival of thought, as Valéry said. Bergson saw this. If man arises in the midst of the world and transforms the automatisms of nature, he owes it, according to Bergson, to his body, to his brain: "he owes it to his language which furnishes consciousness with an immaterial body in which it can incarnate itself." In and through language it is generally the expression with which Bergson is concerned. He saw that philosophy did not consist in realizing freedom and matter, spirit and body apart from one another or in opposing them. In order to be themselves, freedom and spirit must witness themselves in matter or in the body; that is to say, they must express themselves. "It is a question," he says in *Creative Evolution*, "of creating with matter, which is pure necessity, an instrument of freedom, of fabricating a mechanism which will triumph over mechanism." Matter is an obstacle, but it is also an instrument and a stimulus. It is as if the spirit which, from the beginning, hovered over the waters had need of constructing for itself the instruments of its manifestation in order to exist completely.

What we call expression is only another formula for the phenomenon to which Bergson continually returns—the retroactive effect of the true. The experience of the true cannot keep from projecting itself back into the time which preceded it. Frequently this is only an anachronism and an *illusion*. But in *Thought and Movement* Bergson suggests, in speaking of a *retrograde movement of the true*, that it is a question of a fundamental property of truth. To think, or, in other words, to think an idea as true, implies that we arrogate to ourselves the right of recovering the past, either to treat it as an anticipation of the present, or at least to place the past and the present in the same world. What I say of the sensible world is not in the sensible world, and yet it has no other meaning than to say what the sensible world means. The expression antedates itself and postulates that being comes towards it. This exchange between the past and the present, between matter and spirit, silence and speech, the world and us, this metamorphosis of one into the other, with a transparent gleam of truth, is, in our view, much more than the famous intuitive coincidence, the best of Bergsonism.

A philosophy of this kind understands its own strangeness, for it is never entirely in the world, and yet never outside the world. Expression presupposes someone who expresses, a truth which he expresses, and the others before whom he expresses himself. The postulate of expression and of philosophy is that it can simultaneously satisfy these three conditions. Philosophy cannot be a tête-à-tête of the philosopher with the true. It cannot be a judgment given from on high on life, the world, history, as if the philosopher *was not part of it*—nor can it subordinate the internally recognized truth to any exterior instance of it. It must go beyond this alternative.

Bergson understood this well. After declaring in his testament of 1937 that his reflexions had "led him closer and closer to catholicism," he added these words which pose our problem: "I would have been converted if I had not seen for many years the beginnings of the fearsome wave of antisemitism which was about to break out in the world. I have wished to remain among those who tomorrow will be the persecuted." We know that he kept his word even to the point of refusing, in spite of sickness and age, the favors which a power, ashamed of its own principles, wanted to give to this illustrious Jew. Therefore no secret baptism, in spite of the legend, and in spite of his assent on fundamentals. It is here that we see how Bergson conceived our relation to truth. The assent to truths borne by an institution or a church could not release him from this pact of history which he had made with the persecuted of tomorrow. His conversion would have been a desertion, and an open adherence to Christianity could not prevail over the God who was hidden in the sufferings of the persecuted.

We can say: if the philosopher truly thinks that a church holds the secrets of life and the instruments of salvation, he cannot better serve others than by serving it without reservations. But this is doubtless a vain hypothesis. By the very choice he made, Bergson attested that, for him, there is no *place of truth* to which one should go to search for it at any cost, even breaking human relationships and the ties of life and history. Our relationship to the true passes through others. Either we go towards the true with them, or it is not towards the true that we are going. But the real difficulty is that, if the true is not an idol, the others in their turn are not gods. There is no truth without them, but it does not suffice to attain to the truth to be with them. At the time when he was being earnestly asked finally to write his ethics, Bergson wrote a little phrase which shows this well: "one is never obliged to write a book." We cannot expect a philosopher to go beyond what he sees himself, or to give precepts of which he is not sure. The impatience of others is not an argument here; one does not serve others by the more-or-less or by imposture. Thus it is the philosopher and he alone who is judge.

Here we have come back to the self and to the tête-à-tête of the self with the true. Now we have said that there is no solitary truth. Are we therefore on a revolving wheel? We are, but it is not the wheel of the skeptics. It is true that in the last resort there is no judge, that I do not think according to the true alone, nor according to myself alone, nor according to the others alone, because each of the three has need of the other two and it would be a non-sense to sacrifice any one. A philosophical life always bases itself on these three cardinal points. The enigma of philosophy (and of expression) is that sometimes life is the same to oneself, to others, and to the true. These are the moments which justify it. The philosopher counts only on them. He will never accept to will himself against men, nor to will men against himself, nor against the true, nor the true against them. He wishes to be everywhere at once, at the risk of never being completely anywhere. His opposition is not aggressive; he knows that this often announces capitulation. But he understands the rights of others and of the outside too well to permit them any infringement. If, when he is engaged in external enterprises, the attempt is made to draw him beyond the point where his activity loses the meaning which inspired it, his rejection is all the more tranquil in that it is founded on the same motives as his acceptance. Hence the rebellious gentleness, the pensive engagement, the intangible presence which disquiet those who are with him. As Bergson said of Ravaisson in a tone so personal that one imagines him to be speaking of himself: "He gave no hold. . . . He was the kind of man who does not even offer sufficient resistance for one to flatter himself that he has ever seen him give way."

III / Socrates

IF WE HAVE RECALLED these words of Bergson, not all of which are in his books, it is because they make us feel that there is a tension in the relation of the philosopher with other persons or with life, and that this uneasiness is essential to philosophy. We have forgotten this a little. The modern philosopher is frequently a functionary, always a writer, and the freedom allowed him in his books admits an opposite view. What he says enters first of all into an academic world where the choices of life are deadened and the occasions for thought are cut off. Without books a certain speed of communication would be impossible, and there is nothing to say against them.

But in the end they are only words expressed a bit more coherently. The philosophy placed in books has ceased to challenge men. What is unusual and almost insupportable in it is hidden in the respectable life of the great philosophical systems. In order to understand the total function of the philosopher, we must remember that even the philosophical writers whom we read and who we are have never ceased to recognize as their patron a man who never wrote, who never taught, at least in any official chair, who talked with anyone he met on the street, and who had certain difficulties with public opinion and with the public powers. We must remember Socrates.

The life and death of Socrates are the history of the difficult relations that the philosopher faces—when he is not protected by literary immunity—with the gods of the City, that is to say with other men, and with the fixed absolute whose image they extend to him. If the philosopher were a rebel, it would be less shocking. For in the last analysis each one of us knows for his own part that the world as it is, is unacceptable. We like to have this written down for the honor of humanity, though we may forget it when we return to our affairs. Hence rebellion is not displeasing. But with Socrates it is something different. He teaches that religion is true, and he offered sacrifices to the gods. He teaches that one ought to obey the City, and he obeys it from the very beginning to the end. He is reproached not so much for what he does as for his way of doing it, his motive. In the *Apology* there is a saying which explains it all, when Socrates says to his judges: *Athenians, I believe as none of those who accuse me.* Revealing words! He believes *more* than they, but also he believes in another way, and in a different sense. True religion for Socrates is religion in which the gods are not in conflict, where the omens remain ambiguous—since, in the last analysis, says the Socrates of Xenophon, it is the gods, not the birds, who foresee the future—where the divine reveals itself, like the *daimon* of Socrates, only by a silent warning and a reminder to man of his ignorance. Religion is, therefore, true, but true in a sense that it does not know—true as Socrates thinks it, not as it thinks.

And in the same way when he justifies the City, it is for his own reasons, not for *raisons d'Etat.* He does not run away. He appears before the tribunal. But there is little respect in the reasons he gives for this. First of all, he says, at my age the lust for life is not in place; furthermore, one would not put up with me much better elsewhere; finally, I have always lived here. There remains the celebrated argument for the authority of the laws. But we need to examine it more closely. Xenophon makes Socrates say that one may obey the laws in wishing for them to change, as one fights a war in wishing for peace. Thus it is not that the laws are good but that they pertain to order, and one needs order in order to change it. When Socrates refuses to flee, it is not that he recognizes the tribunal. It is that he may be in a better position to challenge it. By fleeing, that is, he would become an enemy of Athens and would make the sentence against him true. By remaining, he has won, whether he be acquitted or condemned, for he will prove his philosophy either in leading his judges to accept it, or in his own acceptance of the sentence.

Aristotle, seventy-five years later, will say, in leaving the city of his own accord, that there is no sense in allowing the Athenians to commit a new crime against philosophy. Socrates, on the other hand, works out for himself another idea of philosophy. It does not exist as a sort of idol of which he would be the guardian and which he must defend. It exists rather in its living relevance to the Athenians, in its absent presence, in its obedience without respect. Socrates has a way of obeying which is a way of resisting, while Aristotle disobeys in seemliness and dignity. Everything that Socrates does is ordered around the secret principle that one is annoyed if he does not comprehend. Always to blame by excess or default, always more simple and yet less abstract than the others, more flexible and less accommodating, he makes them ill at ease, and inflicts upon them the unpardonable offense of making them doubt themselves. He is there in life, at the assembly of the people, and before the tribunal, but in such a way that one can make nothing of him. He gives them no eloquence, no prepared rhetoric. By entering into the game of respect, he would only justify the calumny against him. But even less any show of defiance! This would be to forget that in a certain sense the others can hardly judge otherwise than they do. The same philosophy obliges him to appear before the judges and also makes him different from them. The same freedom which brings him among them frees him from their prejudices. The very same principle makes him both universal and singular. There is a part of him by which he is the kinsman of them all. It is called *reason* and is invisible to them. For them, as Aristophanes says, it is cloudy, empty chattering. The commentators sometimes say it is all a misunderstanding. Socrates believes in religion and the City, in spirit and in truth. They believe in them to the letter. He and his judges are not *on the same ground.* If only he had been better understood, one would have seen clearly that he was neither seeking for new gods, nor neglecting the gods of Athens. He was only trying to give them a sense; he was interpreting them.

The trouble is that this operation is not so innocent. It is in the world of the philosopher that one saves the gods and the laws by understanding them, and to make room on earth for the life of philosophy, it is precisely philosophers like Socrates who are required. Religion interpreted—this is for the others

religion suppressed. And the charge of impiety—
this is the point of view of the others towards him.
He gives reasons for obeying the laws. But it is already too much to have reasons for obeying, since
over against all reasons other reasons can be opposed, and then respect disappears. What one ex-
pects of him—this is exactly what he is not able to
give—is assent to the thing itself, without restriction. He, on the contrary, comes before the judges,
yes, but it is to explain to them what the City is. As
if they did not know! As if they *were not* the City!
He does not plead for himself. He pleads the cause
of a city which would accept philosophy. He reverses
the roles and says to them: it is not myself I am
defending; it is you. In the last analysis the City is
in him and they are the enemies of the laws. It is
they who are being judged, and he who is judging
them—an inevitable reversal in the philosopher,
since he justifies what is outside by values which
come from within.

What can one do if he neither pleads his cause
nor challenges to combat? One can speak in such a
way as to make freedom show itself in and through
the various respects and considerations, and to un-
lock hate by a smile—a lesson for our philosophy
which has lost both its smile and its sense of tragedy.
This is what is called irony. The irony of Socrates
is a distant but true relation with others. It expresses the fundamental fact that each of us is only

himself inescapably, and nevertheless recognizes himself in the other. It is an attempt to open up both of us for freedom. As is true of tragedy, both the adversaries are justified, and true irony uses a double-meaning which is founded on these facts. There is therefore no self-conceit. It is irony on the self no less than on the others. As Hegel well says, it is *naive*. The irony of Socrates is not to say less in order to win an advantage in showing great mental power, or in suggesting some esoteric knowledge. "Whenever I convince anyone of his ignorance," the *Apology* says with melancholy, "my listeners imagine that I know everything that he does not know." Socrates does not know any *more* than they know. He knows only that there is no absolute knowledge, and that it is by this absence that we are open to the truth.

To this good irony Hegel opposes a romantic irony which is equivocal, tricky, and self-conceited. It relies on the power which we can use, if we wish, to give any kind of meaning to anything whatsoever. It levels things down; it plays with them and permits anything. The irony of Socrates is not this kind of madness. Or at least if there are traces of bad irony in it, it is Socrates himself who teaches us to correct Socrates. When he says: I make them dislike me and this is the proof that what I say is true, he is wrong on the basis of his own principles. All sound reasoning is offensive, but all that offends us is not

true. At another time, when he says to his judges: I
will not stop philosophizing *even if I must die many
times,* he taunts them and tempts their cruelty.
Sometimes it is clear that he yields to the giddiness
of insolence and spitefulness, to self-magnification
and the aristocratic spirit. He was left with no other
resource than himself. As Hegel says again, he appeared "at the time of the decadence of the Athe-
nian democracy; he drew away from the externally
existent and retired into himself to seek there for the
just and the good." But in the last analysis it was precisely this that he was self-prohibited from doing,
since he thought that one cannot be just all alone
and, indeed, that in being just all alone one ceases
to be just. If it is truly the City that he is defending,
it is not merely the City in him but that actual City
existing around him. The five hundred men who
gathered together to judge him were neither all important people nor all fools. Two hundred and
twenty-one among them thought he was innocent,
and a change of thirty votes would have saved
Athens from the dishonor. It was also a question of
those after Socrates who would run the same danger.
He was perhaps free to bring down the anger of the
fools upon himself, to pardon them with a certain
contempt, and then to pass beyond his life. But this
would not absolve him in advance from the evil he
might bring on others and would not enable him to
pass beyond *their* lives. It was therefore necessary

to give to the tribunal its chance of understanding. In so far as we live with others, no judgment we make on them is possible which leaves us out, and which places them at a distance. *All is vain,* or *all is evil,* as likewise *all is well,* which are hard to distinguish, do not come from philosophy.

IV / Religion

IT IS POSSIBLE TO FEAR that our time also is rejecting the philosopher that dwells within it, and that once again philosophy will evaporate into nothing but *clouds.* For to philosophize is to seek, and this is to imply that there are things to see and to say. Well, today we no longer seek. We "return" to one or the other of our traditions and "defend" it. Our convictions are founded less on perceived values and truths than on the vices and errors of those we do not like. We love very few things, though we dislike many. Our thinking is a thought in retreat or in reply. Each of us is expiating for his youth. This decadence is in accord with the course of our history. Having passed a certain point of tension, ideas cease to develop and live. They fall to the level of justifications and pretexts, relics of the past, points of honor; and what one pompously calls the movement of ideas is reduced to the sum of our nostalgias, our grudges, our timidities, and our phobias. In this world, where negation and gloomy passion take the place of certitude, one does not seek above all to see, and, because it seeks to see, philosophy passes for impiety. It would be easy to show this in connection with two absolutes which are at the center of our discussions: God and history.

It is striking to find that today one no longer proves the existence of God, as Saint Thomas, Saint Anselm, and Descartes did. The proofs are ordinarily presupposed, and one limits one's self to refuting the negation of God either by seeking to find some gap in the new philosophies through which the constantly presupposed notion of the necessary being may be made to reappear or, if these philosophies place this notion decidedly in question, by abruptly disqualifying them as *atheism*. Even such relatively serene reflections as those of Father de Lubac on atheistic humanism, and those of M. Maritain on the meaning of contemporary atheism are carried on as if philosophy, when it is not theological, is reduced to the negation of God. Father de Lubac takes as the object of his study an atheism which truly wishes, he says, "to replace what it destroys," which, therefore, begins by destroying what it wishes to replace, and which is rather, like that of Nietzsche, a sort of deicide. Maritain examines what he rather curiously calls positive atheism, and which soon comes to appear to him as an "active combat against everything that suggests God," an "antitheism," an "act of inverted faith," a "refusal of God," a "defiance against God." This antitheism certainly exists, but since it is an inverted theology, it is not a philosophy, and by focusing the whole discussion on it, one shows perhaps that it holds locked up within itself the very theology it is attacking. But at the same time one reduces everything to a controversy between theism and anthropotheism as they re-echo the troubles of religious alienation, and forgets to ask whether the philosopher really has to choose either the theology and the apocalypse of Wonderland or the "mystique of the superman," and whether any philosopher has ever endowed man with the metaphysical functions of omnipotence.

Philosophy works itself out in another order, and it is for the same reasons that it eludes both Promethean humanism and the rival affirmations of theology. The philosopher does not say that a final transcendence of human contradictions may be possible, and that the complete man awaits us in the future. Like everyone else, he knows nothing of this. He says—and this is something altogether different —that the world is going on, that we do not have to judge its future by what has happened in the past, that the idea of a destiny in things is not an idea but a dizziness, that our relations with nature are not fixed once and for all, that no one can know what freedom may be able to do, nor imagine what our customs and human relations would be in a civilization no longer haunted by competition and necessity. He does not place his hope in any destiny, even a favorable one, but in something belonging to us which is precisely not a destiny—in the contingency of our history. The denial of this is a fixed (non-philosophical) position.

Must we then say that the philosopher is a humanist? No, if one understands by "man" an explanatory principle which ought to be substituted for the others. One explains nothing by man, since he is not a force but a weakness at the heart of being, a cosmological factor, but also the place where all cosmological factors, by a mutation which is never finished, change in sense and become history. Man is as effective in the contemplation of an inhuman nature as in the love of himself. His existence extends to too many things, in fact to all, for him to become the object of his own delight, or for the authorization of what we can now reasonably call a "human chauvinism." This same wide-ranging flexibility, which eludes every religion of humanity, also takes the wind from the sails of theology. For theology recognizes the contingency of human existence only to derive it from a necessary being, that is, to remove it. Theology makes use of philosophical wonder only for the purpose of motivating an affirmation which ends it. Philosophy, on the other hand, arouses us to what is problematic in our own existence and in that of the world, to such a point that we shall never be cured of searching for a solution, as Bergson says, "in the notebooks of the master."

Father de Lubac discusses an atheism which means to suppress this searching, he says, "even including the problem as to what is responsible for the birth of God in human consciousness." This problem is so little ignored by the philosopher that, on the contrary, he radicalizes it, and places it above the "solutions" which stifle it. The idea of necessary being, as well as that of "eternal matter" and "total man," appear prosaic to him in comparison with this constant manifesting of religious phenomena through all the stages of world history, and this continual rebirth of the divine which he is trying to describe. In this situation, he is well able to understand religion as one of the expressions of the central phenomenon of consciousness. But the example of Socrates reminds us that it is not the same thing, but almost the opposite, to understand religion and to accept it. Lichtenberg, of whom Kant said that each of his phrases hid a profound thought, held something of the following kind: one should neither affirm the existence of God nor deny it. As he explained: "it is not necessary that doubt should be anything more than vigilance; otherwise, it can become a source of danger." It is not that he wished merely to leave certain perspectives open, nor to please everyone. It is rather that he was identifying himself, for his part, with a consciousness of self, of the world, and of others that was "strange" (the word is his) in a sense which is equally well destroyed by the rival explanations.

This decisive moment when certain particles of matter, words, and events allow themselves to be animated by a meaning, the nearest contours of which they suggest without containing, is above all the fundamental keynote of the world which is already given with the least of our perceptions. Both consciousness and history echo this. It is the same thing to establish them against any naturalistic explanation as it is to release them from any sovereign necessity. Hence one bypasses philosophy when one *defines* it as atheism. This is philosophy as it is seen by the theologian. Its negation is only the beginning of an attention, a seriousness, an experience on the basis of which it must be judged. Furthermore, if one remembers the history of the word *atheism,* and how it has been applied even to Spinoza, the most positive of philosophers, we must admit that all thinking which displaces, or otherwise defines, the sacred has been called atheistic, and that philosophy which does not place it here or there, like a thing, but at the joining of things and words, will always be exposed to this reproach without ever being touched by it.

A sensitive and open thought should not fail to guess that there is an affirmative meaning and even a presence of the spirit in this philosophical nega-

tivity. Indeed Maritain finally comes to justify the
continuous criticism of idols as essential to Christianity. The saint, he says, is a "complete atheist" with
respect to a God who would be only the guarantor of
the natural order, who would consecrate not only all
the world's goodness but all the world's evil as well,
who would justify slavery, injustice, the tears of
children, the agony of the innocent by sacred neces-
sities, who would finally sacrifice man to the cosmos
as "the absurd Emperor of the world." The Christian
God who redeems the world and is accessible to
prayer, according to Maritain, is the active negation
of all this. Here, indeed, we are close to the essence
of Christianity. The philosopher will only ask himself
if the natural and rational concept of God as necessary being is not inevitably that of the Emperor of
the world, if without this concept, the Christian God
would not cease to be the author of the world, and
if the criticism we are now suggesting is not the
philosophy which presses to the limit that criticism
of false gods which Christianity has introduced into
our history? Yes, *where* will one stop the criticism of
idols, and *where* will one ever be able to say the true
God actually resides if, as Maritain writes, we pay
tribute to false gods "every time we bow before the
world"?

V / History

In considering the other theme of contemporary discussion, history, one may see that here again philosophy seems to despair of itself. Some see in history an external destiny for the sake of which the philosopher is invited to suppress himself as philosopher. Others maintain that philosophy is autonomous, but only by detaching it from concrete circumstances, and by making of it an honorable alibi. One *defends* philosophy and one *defends* history as though they were rival traditions. The founders who lived these traditions found no great difficulty in bringing them to coexist in themselves. For taken in their original condition, in human practice, they do not divide into opposed alternatives. They advance and decline together.

Hegel had already identified them, by making philosophy the understanding of historical experience, and history the becoming of philosophy. But the conflict was only masked, since for Hegel philosophy is absolute knowledge, system, totality, whereas the history of which the philosopher speaks is not really history, that is to say, something which one does. It is rather universal history, fully comprehended, finished, dead. But, on the other hand, history as pure fact or event, introduces into the system in which it is incorporated an internal movement which tears it to pieces. These two points of view both remain true for Hegel, and we know that he carefully maintained this equivocation. At certain times he makes the philosopher appear as the simple reader of a history already accomplished, as the owl of Minerva who takes flight only at dusk, when the work of history is finished. But at other times he seems to make the philosopher the only subject of history, since he alone does not undergo it, but comprehends it by elevating it to the level of the concept. In reality this equivocation works to the profit of the philosopher. Since history has been staged by him, he finds in it only the sense he has already placed there, and in accepting it he merely accepts himself. It is to Hegel, perhaps, that we should apply what Alain has said of the subtler merchants of sleep who "offer us a sleep in which the dreams are precisely the world in which we live." The universal history of Hegel is the dream of history. As in our dreams, all that is thought is real, and all that is real is thought. There is nothing at all for men to do who are not already taken up in the system. The philosopher does in fact make a certain concession to them. He admits that he is not able to think of anything that has not already been done, thus granting to them the monopoly of efficient action. But since he reserves the monopoly of meaning to himself, it is in the philosopher, and in him alone, that history makes sense. It is the philosopher who thinks and who decrees the identity of history and philosophy —which is to say in other words that there is no such thing.

The novelty of Marx, as a critic of Hegel, was, therefore, not to identify the mover of history with human productivity, nor to interpret philosophy as a reflection of historical movement, but rather to denounce the trick by which the philosopher slips the system into history in order then to recover it and to reaffirm its omnipotence precisely at the moment when he seemed to give it up. Even the privilege of speculative philosophy, the claim of philosophical existence, as the young Marx said, to take up all the other forms of existence, is itself a historical fact, not the bringing to birth of history. Marx himself discovers a historical rationality immanent in the life of men. For him, history is not merely the order of fact or of reality on which philosophy, with its rationality, will confer the right to exist. History is rather the situation in which all meanings are developed, and in particular the conceptual meanings of philosophy, in so far as they are legitimate. What Marx calls *praxis* is the meaning which works itself out spontaneously in the intercrossing of those activities by which man organizes his relations with nature and with other men. It is not directed at the beginning by an idea of universal or total history. We must remember that Marx insisted on the impossibility of thinking the future. It is rather the analysis of the past and present which enables us to perceive in outline a logic in the course of things which does not so much guide it from the outside as emanate from within it, and which will be achieved only if men understand their experience, and will to change it. From the course of things we know only that sooner or later it will eliminate the irrational historical forms which secrete ferments that will destroy them. This elimination of the irrational can lead to chaos, if the forces destroying these forms do not show themselves capable of constructing something new out of them. Hence there is no universal history. Perhaps we shall never advance beyond pre-history. Historical meaning is immanent in the interhuman event, and is as fragile as this event. But precisely because of this, the event takes on the value of a genesis of reason. Philosophy no longer has the power of exhaustive comprehension which Hegel gave it. But also it can no longer be, as with Hegel, the mere reflection of a history that is past. As the young Marx said at another time, one "destroys" philosophy as a detached mode of knowing, only to "realize" it in actual history. Rationality passes from the concept to the heart of interhuman *praxis*, and certain historical facts take on a metaphysical meaning. Philosophy lives in these facts.

In denying to philosophical thought the power of

exhaustive comprehension, Marx is not able, as his successors and perhaps he himself believed, to turn the dialectic of consciousness into a dialectic of matter, or things. When a man says that there is a dialectic in things, this can mean only in things so far as he thinks them, and such objectivity, as the example of Hegel shows, is the height of subjectivism. Marx, therefore, does not transfer the dialectic into things; he transforms it into men, understood of course with all their human equipment as being engaged, through work and culture, in an enterprise which transforms nature and social relations. Philosophy is not an illusion. It is the algebra of history. Furthermore, the contingency of human events is no longer understood as a defect in the logic of history, but rather as its condition. Without such contingency there would be only a phantom of history. If one knows where history is going inevitably, events taken one by one have neither importance nor meaning. The future is already ripe, whatever happens. Nothing is truly at stake in the present, since whatever it may be, it is proceeding towards the same future. On the contrary, whoever thinks that there is something preferable in the present implies that the future is contingent. History has no meaning, if this meaning is understood as that of a river which, under the influence of all-powerful causes, flows towards an ocean in which it disappears. Every appeal to universal history cuts off the meaning of the specific event, renders effective history insignificant, and is a nihilism in disguise. As an external God is *ipso facto* a false God, so an external history is no longer history. The two rival absolutes live only if, in full being, a human project which challenges them is opened up. It is in history that philosophy learns to know this philosophical negativity, to which one vainly opposes the finished completeness of history.

If the followers of Marx hardly understood him, and if he himself, after his youthful writings, ceased to understand himself in this way, it was because his original insight into *praxis* put in question the usual categories of philosophy, and because nothing in sociology and in positive history was preparing the way for the intellectual reform which he called for. Where, in fact, was this immanent meaning of inter-human events to be placed? It is not, or certainly it is not always, in men, that is, in their minds, but outside them. Once we had stopped placing any absolute knowledge in things, it seemed that there were only blind events. *Where* then was the histori-cal process, and what mode of existence must be recognized in such historical forms as feudalism, capitalism, proletariat, which are spoken of as though they were persons, knowing and willing, hidden behind the multiplicity of events, without seeing clearly what these masks [*prosopopées*] rep-resent? After rejecting the expedient of the Hegelian Objective Spirit, how could the dilemma of existence as thing versus existence as consciousness be avoided? How could one understand the generalized meaning which works in these historical forms and in the whole of history, which is not the thought of any one mind but which appeals to all? The simplest possibility was to imagine vaguely a dialectic of matter, whereas Marx, on the contrary, spoke of a "human matter," held, that is, in the movement of *praxis*. But this expedient altered the intuition of Marx. In relation to the dialectic of things, all philosophy fell to the rank of ideology, illusion, or even of mystification. One lost all means of knowing whether, as Marx intended, philosophy was finally realized in its destruction, or whether it was simply made to disappear—to say nothing of the injuries suffered by the concept of history.

As often happens with philosophical insights, the union of philosophy and history lives again in more recent and special investigations which, though not directly inspired by Hegel and Marx, retrace their steps because they confront the very same difficulties. The theory of signs, as developed in linguistics, perhaps implies a conception of historical meaning which gets beyond the opposition of *things* versus *consciousness*. Living language is precisely that togetherness of thinking and thing which causes the difficulty. In the act of speaking, the subject, in his tone and in his style, bears witness to his autonomy, since nothing is more proper to him, and yet at the same moment, and without contradiction, he is turned towards the linguistic community and is dependent on his language. The will to speak is one and the same as the will to be understood. The presence of the individual in the institution, and of the institution in the individual is evident in the case of linguistic change. It is often the wearing down of a form which suggests to us a new way of using the means of discrimination which are present in the language at a given time. The constant need for communication leads us to invent and to accept a new usage which is not deliberate and yet which is systematic. The contingent fact, taken over by the will to expression, becomes a new means of expression which takes its place, and has a lasting sense in the history of this language. In such cases, there is a rationality in the contingent, a lived logic, a self-constitution of which we have definite need in trying to understand the union of contingency and meaning in history, and Saussure, the modern linguist, could have sketched a new philosophy of history.

The reciprocal relations between the will to express and the means of expression correspond to those between the productive forces and the forms of production, and more generally, between historical forces and institutions. Just as language is a system of signs which have meaning only in relation to one another, and each of which has its own usage throughout the whole language, so each institution is a symbolic system that the subject takes over and incorporates as a style of functioning, as a global configuration, without having any need to conceive it at all. When equilibrium is destroyed, the reorganizations which take place comprise, like those of language, an internal logic even though it may not be clearly thought out by anyone. They are polarized by the fact that, as participants in a system of symbols, we exist in the eyes of one another, with one another, in such a way that changes in language are due to our will to speak and to be understood. The system of symbols affects the molecular changes which occur where a meaning develops, a meaning which is neither a thing nor an idea, in spite of the famous dichotomy, because it is a modulation of our coexistence. It is in this way, as is also true of logics of behavior, that the forms and processes of history, the classes, the epochs, exist. We were asking ourselves where they are. They are in a social, cultural, or symbolic space which is no less real than physical space and is, moreover, supported by it. For meaning lies latent not only in language, in political and religious institutions, but in modes of kinship, in machines, in the landscape, in production, and, in general, in all the modes of human commerce. An interconnection among all these phenomena is possible, since they are all symbolisms, and perhaps even the translation of one symbolism into another is possible.

What is the situation of philosophy with respect to a history thus conceived? Each philosophy is also an architecture of signs. It constitutes itself in close relation with the other modes of exchange which make up our historical and social life. Philosophy is in history, and is never independent of historical discourse. But for the tacit symbolism of life it substitutes, in principle, a conscious symbolism; for a latent meaning, one that is manifest. It is never content to accept its historical situation (as it is not content to accept its own past). It changes this situation by revealing it to itself and, therefore, by giving it the opportunity of entering into conversation with other times and other places where its truth appears. Hence it is no more possible to set up a one-to-one correspondence between the historical event and the conscious philosophical interpretations of this event, than between the event and its objective conditions. The book, if it is authentic, transcends itself as a dated event. Philosophical, aesthetic, and literary criticism, therefore, have an intrinsic value, and history can never take their place. It is also true, however, that one can always recover from the book the fragments of history on which it has crystallized, and this is really necessary in order to know to what extent it has changed them in their truth. Philosophy turns towards the anonymous symbolic activity from which we emerge, and towards the personal discourse which develops in us, and which, indeed, we are. It scrutinizes this power of expression which the other forms of symbolism exercise only in a limited way. In touch with every kind of fact and experience, it tries rigorously to grasp those fecund moments in which a meaning takes possession of itself. It recovers this meaning, and also pushes beyond all limits the becoming of truth, which presupposes and brings it about that there is only one history and one world.

VI / Philosophy

Let us show, in conclusion, that views like these justify philosophy even in its weakness.

For it is useless to deny that philosophy limps. It dwells in history and in life, but it wishes to dwell at their center, at the point where they come into being with the birth of meaning. It is not content with what is already there. Since it is expression in act, it comes to itself only by ceasing to coincide with what is expressed, and by taking its distance in order to see its meaning. It is, in fact, the Utopia of possession at a distance. Hence it can be tragic, since it has its own contrary within itself. It is never a *serious* occupation. The serious man, if he exists, is the man of one thing only, to which he assents. But the most resolute philosophers always wish the contrary—to realize, but in destroying; to suppress, but also to conserve. Always, they have an afterthought. The philosopher pays attention to the serious man— of action, of religion, or of passion—perhaps more acutely than anyone. But precisely in doing this, one feels that he is different. His own actions are acts of witness, like the "signifying acts" by which the companions of Julien Sorel at the seminary sought to prove their piety. Spinoza writes *"ultimi barbarorum"* on the tyrants' gate. Lagneau took legal action before the University authorities to rehabilitate an unfortunate candidate. Having done these things, each returns home, and remains there for years. The philosopher of action is perhaps the farthest removed from action, for to speak of action with depth and rigor is to say that one does not desire to act.

Machiavelli is the complete contrary of a machiavellian, since he describes the tricks of power and, as we say, "gives the whole show away." The seducer and the politician, who live in the dialectic and have a feeling or instinct for it, try their best to keep it hidden. It is the philosopher who explains that dialectically, under given conditions, an opponent becomes the equivalent of a traitor. This language is the precise opposite of what the powers say. The powers omit the premisses and speak more succinctly. They simply say: here there are nothing but criminals. The manichees, who throw themselves into action, understand one another better than they understand the philosopher, for there is a certain complicity among them. Each one is the reason for the being of the other. But the philosopher is a stranger to this fraternal melée. Even if he had never betrayed any cause, one feels, in his very manner of being faithful, that he would be able to betray. He does not take sides like the others, and in his assent something massive and carnal is lacking. He is not altogether a real being.

This difference exists. But is it really between the philosopher and the man? It is rather the difference in man himself between that which understands and that which chooses, and every man, like the philosopher, is divided in this way. There is much that is artificial in the portrait of the man of action whom we oppose to the philosopher. This man of action is himself not all of one piece. Hate is a virtue from behind. To obey with one's eyes closed is the beginning of panic; and to choose against what one understands, the beginning of skepticism. One must be able to withdraw and gain distance in order to become truly engaged, which is, also, always an engagement in the truth. The same author who wrote one day that all action is manichean, having become involved in action soon after, familiarly answered a journalist who reminded him of what he had said: "all action is manichean, *but don't overdo it!*"

No one is manichean before himself. It is an air that men of action have when seen from the outside, and which they rarely treasure in their memories.

If the philosopher helps us to understand, hence-forth, something of what a great man says in his own heart, he saves the truth for all, even for the man of action, who needs it, for no real statesman has ever seriously said that he was not interested in the truth. Later on, perhaps tomorrow, the man of action will rehabilitate the philosopher. As for those who are simply men, and not professionals in action, they are very far from classifying all others into the good and the evil, at least as long as they speak of what they have seen, and judge from close up. One finds them, when one looks, to be surprisingly sensitive to philosophical irony, as if it brought their silence and their reserve into the light, because here, for once, the word serves to open and release us.

The limping of philosophy is its virtue. True irony is not an alibi; it is a task; and the very detachment of the philosopher assigns to him a certain kind of action among men. Because we live in one of those situations that Hegel called diplomatic, in which every initiative risks being changed in meaning, we sometimes believe that we are serving the cause of philosophy by isolating it from the problems of the day, and Descartes has recently been honored for not having taken sides between Galileo and the Holy Office. The philosopher, it is said, should not prefer one rival dogmatism to another. He should occupy himself with absolute being beyond both the object of the physicist and the imagination of the theologian. But this is to forget that, by refusing to speak, Descartes also refuses to vindicate and to bring into action the philosophical order in its proper place. By remaining silent, he does not transcend these twin errors. He leaves them at grips with one another; he encourages them, particularly the victor of the moment. To be silent is not the same as to say why one does not wish to choose. If Descartes had acted, he could not have failed to establish the relative right of Galileo against the Holy Office, even if this were finally to subordinate ontology to physics. Philosophy and absolute being are never above the rival errors that oppose each other at any given time. These are never errors in quite the same way, and philosophy, which is integral truth, is charged with saying what in them it is able to integrate. In order that one day there might be a state of the world in which free thought would be possible, of scientism as well as of imagination, it did not suffice to bypass these two errors in silence. It was essential to speak against, and in this case to speak against the imagination. In the case of Galileo, the thought of physics carried the interests of truth. The philosophical absolute does not have any permanent seat. It is never elsewhere; it must be defended in each event. Alain said to his students: "Truth is momentary for us men who have a short view. It belongs to a situation, to an instant; it is necessary to see it, to say it, to do it at this very moment, not before nor after in ridiculous maxims; not for many times, for there are no many times." The difference here is not between the man and the philosopher. Both of them think the truth in the event. They are both opposed to the important one who thinks by principles, and against the roué who lives without truth.

At the conclusion of a reflection which at first isolates him, the philosopher, in order to experience more fully the ties of truth which bind him to the world and history, finds neither the depth of himself nor absolute knowledge, but a renewed image of the world and of himself placed within it among others. His dialectic, or his ambiguity, is only a way of putting into words what every man knows well— the value of those moments when his life renews itself and continues on, when he gets hold of himself again, and understands himself by passing beyond, when his private world becomes the common world. These mysteries are in each one of us as in him. What does he say of the relation between the soul and the body, except what is known by all men who make their souls and bodies, their good and their evil, go together in one piece? What does he teach of death, except that it is hidden in life, as the body in the soul, and that it is this understanding, as Montaigne said, which brings "a peasant and whole peoples to die, just as surely as philosophers?" The philosopher is the man who wakes up and speaks. And man contains silently within himself the paradoxes of philosophy, because to be completely a man, it is necessary to be a little more and a little less than man.

Author's Notes

NOTE I

This double movement can be noted in his reflections on death and immortality—problems, he thought, which put to the test all our analyses of the relation between mind and the world. Lavelle was opposed to conceptions which would make of death a simple break between life in the relative and life in the absolute, and of immortality, a prolonging of life, or, as he said, the "tomorrow after death." When he spoke of immortality, he did not say that death is nothing and that life continues after it, but, on the contrary, that by death the subject passes into another mode of being. Freed from dispersion and alienation, concentrated in himself, changed in essence, he is, for the first time, fully that which he has never been able to be, except imperfectly. Life was, therefore, a sort of deficient eternity, the seal of the eternal being stamped only on a terminated existence. Life was the vigil of death. Indeed, in certain passages of *l'Ame humaine*, the terminal event is "incorporated in our souls." Death gives "to all events which precede it that mark of the absolute which they would never possess if they were not going to be suddenly interrupted." The absolute inhabits each of our enterprises, in so far as it is done once and for all, and will never begin again. It comes to our life in virtue of its very temporality. Thus the eternal becomes fluid, and flows back from the end into the heart of life. Death is no longer the truth of life, and life is no longer the waiting for that moment when we will be changed in our essence. What is always unfinished, deficient, and cramped in the present is no longer a sign of a lesser reality. But, then, the truth of a being is not its essence, or what it has finally become. It is rather its existence, its active becoming. And if, as Lavelle used to say, we believe ourselves to be closer to the dead we have loved than to the living, this is because they no longer place us in question, and because, from now on, we can dream of them as we choose. Such piety is not far from being impious. The only memory which respects them is the one which maintains the actual use they have made of themselves and of their world, the accent of their freedom in the incompleteness of their lives. The same fragile principle makes us alive, and also gives to what we do a sense that does not wear out.

NOTE II

It must be noted even now that instead of a dialectic of time and space, in Bergson it is often a question of a sort of contamination of time by space, as when he speaks of "attributing material extension to perception." The truth is that one never knows whether Bergson is bringing *durée* down into matter and relaxing it in such a way as to destroy it as *durée,* or whether he is making of matter, and of the world, a system of symbols in which the *durée* realizes itself. His thought is not clear on this point, because he did not see the two alternatives. Assuming a "super-consciousness" as the source of both matter and consciousness, he believed he was justified in saying that matter is "like a consciousness where everything is in balance." The strange solidarity of space and *durée,* of things and consciousness, which he found in us, was only the result of their common origin. As for us, we receive their mediation already fully accomplished. Having accepted the paradox of an external expression of the spirit once and for all, and even before we appear on the scene, we need only to describe *extension,* as Bergson says in a significant phrase, "without further scruples." It is precisely under cover of this cosmology that Bergson was able to develop his intuition of the concrete relations between the *durée* and space, spirit and body, without perceiving that this makes the idea of a super-consciousness, or a bodiless spirit, very difficult. In this manner, his philosophy conceals from itself the very problem on the basis of which it was constructed.

NOTE III

It is true that this reading of a life which, as he said of painting, "speaks to our intelligence," led Bergson, before long, to consider it as unmediated. He thought that the painter is himself at the center of his work, and that he possesses "the secret of its physiognomy," although, like all those who struggle with a language, and even more those who create one, the painter does not understand himself as the organizing law of his acts. Bergson was wrong in believing that the picture is "a simple act projected on the canvas," since it is rather the sedimented result of a series of expressive efforts. Without doubt, for him, the phenomenology of life would have been only a preface to the explanation of life by consciousness.

Themes from the Lectures
at the Collège de France
1952-1960

Translated by John O'Neill

1 / The Sensible World and the World of Expression

CONTEMPORARY THINKERS READILY ADMIT that the sensible world and sensible consciousness should be described in terms of what is original to them. But everything continues as though such descriptions did not affect our definition of being and subjectivity. Whenever the higher forms of consciousness and judgment are studied, it is almost always in terms of the thinking subject defined as the pure power of bestowing significations and the capacity of absolute survey. Any attempt to take account of the finitude of sensible consciousness is rejected as a return to naturalism or even pantheism. In contrast, we propose to show that the philosopher learns from his contact with perception an awareness of a relation to being which necessitates and makes possible a new analysis of the understanding. For the meaning of a perceived object when picked out from all others still does not stand isolated from the constellation in which it appears; it is articulated only as a certain *distance* in relation to the order of space, time, motion, and signification in general in which we are established. The meaning of an object is given only as a systematic deformation of our universe of experience, without our ever being able to name its operative principle. Every perception is the perception of something solely by way of being at the same time the relative imperception of a horizon or background which it implies but does not thematize. Perceptual consciousness is therefore indirect or even inverted in relation to an ideal of adequation which it presumes but never encounters directly. Thus if we understand the perceived world as an open field, it would be just as absurd to reduce everything else to this as to impose upon it a "universe of ideas" which owed nothing to it. There is truly a reversal when one passes from the sensible world, in which we are caught, to a world of expression, where we seek to capture significations to serve our purpose, although this reversal and the "retrogressive movement" of truth are solicited by a perceptual anticipation. Properly speaking, the expression which language makes possible resumes and amplifies another expression which is revealed in the "archaeology" of the perceived world.

We have studied the phenomenon of movement as an example of this transition and reversal. There we showed that the simplest perception of movement presupposes a subject who is situated spatially and initiated into the world, and that, from its own side, movement becomes charged with all the meaning scattered in the sensible world and in the silent arts becomes a universal means of expression.

The description of motion as a change in location or variation in the relations between a "mobile" and its coordinates is a retrospective schema, an ulterior formulation of our bodily experience of movement. Once motion is cut off from its perceptual origins, it defies representation and is self-destructive, as has often been shown since Zeno. But to give an intelligible account of motion it is enough to go back, as suggested by Bergson, to the internal experience of motion, in other words, to our *own* movement. We have to understand how the immediate unity of our gesture is able to spread itself over external experiences and introduce into them the possibility of a transition which from the standpoint of objective thought is unreal. We consider the research in Gestalt theory to be valuable for the manner in which it delimits this problem. Thus when two fixed points are projected in succession on a screen they are seen as two traces of a single movement in which they even lose their distinct existence. Here what happens is that the external forces insert themselves into a system of equivalents that is ready to function and in which they operate upon us, like signs in a language, not by arousing their uniquely correspondent significations but, like mileposts, in a process which is still unfolding, or as though they were picking out a path which, as it were, inspired them from a distance. Thus perception is already expression. But this natural language does not isolate; it does not "bring out" what is expressed, but allows it to adhere in its own way more to the "perceptual chain" than to the "verbal chain." When Gestalt theorists show that the perception of motion depends upon numerous *figural moments* and ultimately on the whole structure of the field, they are sketching in the same way as the perceiving subject a sort of *thinking apparatus* which is his incarnate and habitual being. The accomplishment of motion and change of location emanate from a field structure apart from which they are unintelligible. Michotte's studies have shown all the transitions between these configurations and the perception of movement; for example, how the movements of "natation" and "reptation" arise from the very articulation and internal logic of the phonemes. The same order of images, depending upon the cadence in which they follow, can give an observer the impression of a petrified mineral world, or of organic or animal life (Epstein). The quality of the sound from a wind instrument bears the mark and the organic rhythm of the breath from which it came, as can be shown by the strange impression received by reversing the normal register of the sounds. Far from being a simple "displacement," movement is inscribed in the texture of the shapes or qualities and is, so to speak, the revelation of their being. There is, as someone has said, a space and motion of which "the heart is sensible"; their prescription issues from the internal dynamics of the spectacle and reaches a culmination of envelopment in spatial change. The synthesis of perception occurs "on the object" (J. Paliard) [1] and ultimately in the presence of the whole world; it is in and by means of "implication" that the natural light of perception opens its path.

One can only do justice to this allusive relation to being if one undertakes an analysis of the subject who is its source and retraces the birth in him of what is properly called expression. In this task we are aided by contemporary research on the body schema. In these studies the body is the seat of a certain praxis, the point from which there is something to do in the world, the register in which we are inscribed and whose inscription we continue. Such studies renew our conception of space and motion. At every moment the body, as Head has remarked, is a global awareness of distance already covered as well as the means of installing us in advance in the position toward which we are moving (Kohnstamm's phenomenon shows that our arm adopts the position toward which it is moved by muscular forces as though it were already acquired or "normal"). These constant or provisional norms reveal a practical intimacy with space whose relationship to

1. Cf. *Phenomenology of Perception,* trans. Colin Smith (London: Routledge and Kegan Paul; New York: Humanities Press, 1962), pp. 255n, 257n.—*Trans.*

spatial knowledge or gnosis is complex. On the one hand, gnosis is founded upon praxis, since the elementary notions of point, surface, and contour in the last analysis only have meaning for a subject modified by locality and himself situated in the space in which he unfolds the spectacle of a point of view. There is a kind of knowledge that is very close to praxis and can be damaged with it, as is shown in the failure to recognize certain geometric forms in certain apraxia (constructive apraxia). On the other hand, gnosic space is relatively independent of the practical expression of space, as is evident from pathological cases where serious practical impairments are compatible with ability to handle spatial symbols. The relative autonomy of superstructures which outlast the practical conditions which generated them—or can at least for a time hide their collapse—permits us to say with equal truth that we are conscious because we are mobile or that we are mobile because we are conscious. Consciousness, in the sense of knowledge, and movement, in the sense of displacement in objective space, are two abstract moments of a living structure which can very well extend its limits but would also destroy its powers if it were to abolish those limits. Insofar as psychology and psychopathology locate praxis and recognize it as an original domain they are in position to understand the strict relations between mobility and all the symbolic functions as well as to renew our conception of understanding. The analysis of Gerstmann's [2] syndrome (finger agnosia, failure to distinguish left from right, constructive and calculative apraxia) shows the hand to be a "theater where the visual, the linguistic, the spatial, the practical and the constructive seem to converge" (Lange). The body is the vehicle of an indefinite number of symbolic systems whose intrinsic development definitely surpasses the signification in "natural" gestures, but would collapse if ever the body ceases to prompt their operation and install them in the world and our life. Sleep dedifferentiates our praxical functions, beginning with the most subtle, the phonetic system, down to the most elementary, to the point where deep sleep without dreams has been compared to a state of apraxia. Inversely, upon waking the clarity of consciousness restores our diacritical and antithetical systems through which our slumbering relation to the world is quickly disarticulated and annulled. These correlations are examples of the mutation or sublimation which in man transform mobility into symbolic gesticulation and implicit expression into open expression.

As a counter theory, in the last part of the course we outlined the study of movement as a means of universal expression. This theme will be taken up again later (when we will also go into the analysis of linguistic gesticulation which we have

2. J. Gerstmann, "Reine Taktile Agnosie," *Monatsschrift für Psychiatrie und Neurologie*, XLIV (1918), 329–42.— *Trans.*

left aside altogether for another year). We restricted ourselves to examples drawn from the use of movement in painting and cinematic art. Painting does not copy movement point by point or by offering us signs of it; it invents *emblems* which give it a substantial presence, presenting it to us as the "metamorphosis" (Rodin) of one attitude into another, the implication of a future within the present. Now if even change of location can be pictured in this way and be conveyed and understood by symbols which do not move, we can understand how in the history of painting the category of movement develops far beyond simple local displacement. We can see, for example, how pictorial representation, in contrast to lineal representation, can be considered a development of movement in painting. Finally, we speak of movement in painting every time the world is presented indirectly by means of open forms, oblique or partial aspects. From the simplest perception of movement to the experience of painting, we are always faced with the same paradox of a force legible in a form, a trace or signature of time in space. The cinema, invented as a means of photographing objects in movement or as a *representation of movement,* has discovered in the process much more than change in location, namely a new way of symbolizing thoughts, *the movement of representation.* For in the film, in the cutting, editing and changes of perspective, there is a solicitation and, so to speak, a celebration of our openness to the world and to the other person, an openness upon which the film can make continuous variations. The film no longer plays with objective movements, as it did at first, but with changes of perspective which define the shift from one person to another or his merging with the action. In this respect especially, film is still as far as ever from offering us all that we might have expected of it.

Through the study of linguistic symbolism, by taking account of the world of speech as well as the world of expression, we shall be in a position to ascertain definitively the philosophical meaning of the preceding analyses, of the problem of the relation between "natural" expression and cultural expression. We shall then be able to decide whether the dialectic of nature is immanent in our spirit, or whether we should seek a third philosophy beyond this dilemma.

2 / Studies in the Literary Use of Language

For the most part the theory of language confines itself to so-called exact forms, that is to say, to observations about thoughts that have already matured in the person speaking and are at least immanent in the person listening. The result is that such theory loses sight of the heuristic value of language, how it works to gain mastery—which, on the contrary, is clearly seen in the writer at work. Perhaps constituted language should be regarded a secondary form derived from the initial operation which establishes a new signification in a linguistic apparatus constructed with old signs and thus able only to indicate the new meaning or draw the reader and the author himself toward it.

For its own part, literature has been in advance of the interest shown in it by the philosophy of language. For a century now writers have always been more aware of what is singular and even problematic in their calling. Writing is no longer (if it ever was) the simple enunciation of what one has conceived. It is working with a tool which at times produces more and at times less than one has put into it, and this is simply the result of a series of paradoxes that make the writer's craft an exhausting and never-ending task. The paradox of the true and the imaginary, truer than truth—of intentions and achievement, often unexpected and always *other*—of speech and silence, in which expression can fail from being overly deliberate and succeed to the extent that it remains indirect—of the subjective and the objective, in which a writer's deepest secret, still barely articulated inside him, surrenders itself in all clarity to a public which his work creates for itself, while what he possesses most consciously remains by contrast a dead letter—finally, the paradox of the author and the man, where it is evident that it is the man's lived experience which provides the substance of his work and yet, in order *to become true*, needs an elaboration that is the very thing which cuts the writer off from the living community; in other words, all these surprises and traps force literature to see itself as a problem and drive the writer to ask "What is Literature?" [1] thus raising questions not only about his practice but even more about his theory of language. It is this type of question that we have tried to put to the work of Valéry and Stendhal.

1. Jean-Paul Sartre, *What is Literature?* trans. Bernard Frechtman (New York: Harper & Row, 1965).

The use to which Valéry puts language can only be understood if we take into account the long period in which he had killed himself—or wrote only for himself. From the notebooks of 1900 to 1910 (which later formed the two collections *Tel Quel I* and *II*) one can see that his mistrust of language was not just a special case of his distrust of a life which supported itself only by unintelligible prodigies. It is incomprehensible that the body should be both an inert mass which marks our place during sleep and the lively instrument which, for example, in the service of a painter does what it wants to do better than consciousness. It is incomprehensible that the spirit should be a power of doubt, interrogation, reservation, and disengagement which makes us "inalienable" and "unattachable," and at the same time should merge and surrender itself to everything that happens, and that it is precisely by its "indefinite refusal to be anything whatsoever" that it actually constructs and becomes something. It is incomprehensible that I, who am irreducibly alien to all my roles, feel myself moved by my appearance in the gaze of others and that I in turn reflect an image of them that can affect them, so that there is woven between us an "exchange," a "chiasm between two 'destinies' . . ." in which there are never quite two of us and yet one is never alone. These absurdities are most pronounced in language and literature. Language is clear provided one passes over the words quickly enough, but this "fundamental solidity" collapses before a rigorous consciousness. Literature also lives through an imposture: the writer says what his language wants and passes for profound; each lack in him, once it is put into words, becomes a powerful form, and the sum of the accidents which go to make a book appears as the author's intention. At the outset, Valéry could only write "out of weakness" or from cynicism, putting into words all the reasons he had for distrusting words and constructing a work on the negation of all work.

Nevertheless, in the exercise of literature this nihilism is overcome in fact and in principle. However impossible language may have been, it was there. Moreover, there was at least one form of language which one could not reject precisely because it did not pretend *to say something*—namely, poetry. Now, upon examination it became clear that the reason why poetry does not convey signification by effacing itself before what it says, like a plain statement, and is not detached from its words is not simply because poetry is like a song or dance of language, nor is it for want of signification, but it is because it always has more than one signification. Thus it was necessary to admit, at least in the case of poetry, the "miracle" of a "mystical union" of sound and meaning, despite everything we know of the historical accidents that go to make up each language. But once this prodigy has been discovered in poetry in the strict sense, it can be found again in "that endlessly active poetry which torments static language, opening or narrowing the meaning of words, through symmetry or conversions, and which at every moment alters the fiduciary value of this currency." These variations in language, which at first appear to support the skeptic, are ultimately the proof of its meaning, since words would not change in meaning unless they were trying to say something. Thus, relative to a certain state of language—and even if it has to be renewed from one age to another—the attempt to achieve expression has been a success or a failure, either saying something or saying nothing. The justification of poetry rehabilitates the whole of language, and in the end Valéry admits that even the intellectual is not a pure consciousness, illuminated all the more by the refusal to identify with anything whatsoever, and that our clarity comes from our commerce with the world and with others, as we gradually constitute ourselves a system of capacities, which he calls "implex" or "animal of words," that is that hybrid or bastard that guarantees below the level of the will the connection between what we are doing and what we wanted to do. From the contempt of literature as a literary theme there is a transition to a consciously accepted literature, a shift from a definite refusal of any identification whatsoever to the desire to speak and write. "Shall I be on top of my art? I am alive" (*Mon Faust*). Men are "hybrids" of body and spirit, but what is called spirit is inseparable from what is most precarious about them; for light would not illuminate a thing unless there were something to screen it. Precisely because it is radical, the critique of language and life completely merges with the practice of life and language. Valéry's last writings are truly the reply to the crisis of 1892 which led him to the rule of silence; their language sustains its own aim, its own ethic, and its own justification.

Stendhal's is also the story of an apprenticeship to speech. His vital problem, as it appears from the *Journal* for the years 1804 and 1805, lay in his inability, as he puts it, "to feel" and "to perceive" at the same time: on the one hand, he acts self-consciously but cynically and as if role-playing, and he is rightly told that he has not "penetrated" what he said; on the other hand, he surrenders to happiness, but then it is a "reverie" or an ecstasy which deprives him of the strength to go on and leaves him dumb. His first literary essays reveal the same self-misunderstanding; he begins to write for success and to achieve that ambition he relies upon observation almost to the point of a science of life. But unwittingly, and even while he was adopting the Code Civil as his model, he was making an apprenticeship to the inner dialogue in his *Journal*. Once he had given up the promotion of his literary and amatory projects and had opened himself and his writing to the revery he had at first resisted, he suddenly found himself capable of improvisation, conviction, creation. He realized that there is no conflict between truth and fiction, solitude and love, living and writing; and out of the first person, the *ego* which so easily lends itself to slipping into any role, he creates the means of an entirely new art. Henceforth he can consent to himself because in the practice of living and the practice of style he has gained the capacity to escape his separation.

The question remains whether this solution is just a writer's solution which only goes to the improvement of his work, whereas the speaking subject who is open to everything that can be said is, by this very fact, removed from the involvement of life. One could easily believe this on seeing, for example, what little stability Stendhal showed in face of political opinion. Nevertheless, through all the wavering from cynicism to candor, Stendhal did follow a line: he never wavered in his absolute refusal to accept ignorance and misery or in his belief that a man is not formed until he has "settled with reality," until he has escaped from the polite behavior through which his class rules him. Such denials are tantamount to the commitment to a cause. Stendhal is saying roughly that to be human is a political position. Perhaps the function of criticism is the writer's commitment. If it is true, as Stendhal believed, that all power is false, then perhaps we should not overlook the fact that all writers who are unprejudiced and open to the future know what they do not want better than what they do want. Perhaps all men, as well as the man of letters, can only be present to the world and others through language; and perhaps in everyone language is the basic function which constructs a life and its work and transforms even the problems of our existence into life's motives.

3 / The Problem of Speech

SPEECH DOES NOT SIMPLY ACTIVATE the possibilities inscribed in language. Already in Saussure,[1] in spite of his restrictive definitions, speech is far from being a simple effect; it modifies and sustains language just as much as it is conveyed through it. In reality, by adopting speech as his theme, Saussure broke new ground in the study of language and began for us a categorical revision. He challenged the rigid distinction between sign and signification which seemed evident when one considered instituted language alone, but breaks down in speech where sound and meaning are not simply associated. The well-known definition of the sign as "diacritical, oppositive, and negative" means that

1. F. de Saussure, *Cours de linguistique générale* (Paris: Payot, 1964); *Course in General Linguistics*, ed. Charles Bally and Albert Sechehaye with Albert Reidlinger, trans. Wade Baskin (New York: Philosophical Library, 1959).—*Trans.*

language is present in the speaking subject as a
system of intervals between signs and significations,
and that, as a unity, the act of speech simultaneously operates the differentiation of these two orders. Finally, it implies that the distinction between
res extensa and *res cogitans* cannot be applied to
significations that are not closed nor to signs that
exist only in their interrelation.

The purpose of the course is to illustrate and to
extend the Saussurian conception of speech as a
positive and dominating function.

We have first applied it to the problem of the
child's acquisition of language. A Saussurian like
Roman Jakobson readily distinguishes between the
mere factual presence of a sound or phoneme in the
child's babbling and the proper linguistic possession
of the same element as a means of signifying. The
sudden tumble of sounds at the moment the child
begins to speak comes about because, in order to be
at his disposal as means of signification, the child
must integrate the sounds into the system of phonetic contrasts upon which the language surrounding him is constructed and in some sense acquire
the principles of that system. But Jakobson inter-
prets this phenomenon in terms of a debatable psychology. Where the problem is to understand how
the child appropriates the phonetic system and at
the same time is suddenly in possession of the mel-
ody of meaningful language that had previously
"waited for meaning," Jakobson appeals to *attention*
and *judgment*. In other words, Jakobson resorts to

the functions of analysis and judgment, which in reality are dependent upon language and, moreover, inadequately account for the atypical aspect of signs and significations as being due to indiscrimination upon the child's part.

Recently, an advance was made in linking the acquisition of language to the whole series of developments through which the child assumes his surroundings and in particular his relations with others. However, this recourse to the affective context does not *explain* the acquisition of language. In the first place, the developments in the affective decentering are just as enigmatic as the context itself. Secondly, because, above all, language is not just the counterpart or replica of the affective context, it plays a role in it, introducing other motives, changing its internal meaning, and ultimately is itself a form of existence or a diversion within existence. Even subjects who fail to find an effective equilibrium learn to handle the tense of the verb which is supposedly correlated with the various dimensions of their life. The relations with others, intelligence, and language cannot be set out in a lineal and causal series: they belong to those cross-currents where *someone lives*. Speech, said Michelet, is our mother speaking. Thus while speech puts the child in a more profound relation to she who names everything and puts being into words, it also translates this relation into a more general order. The mother opens the child to circuits which from the very beginning flow out from the maternal surrounding which he will never again find through them. The enigma of man and speech is not reduced by "explanations in terms of affectivity." The latter serve only as occasions for the observation of what Freud called the "overdetermination" of speech, transcending "physical language," and for the description of aonther level of interaction between the concrete and the universal, perspective and horizon. The case of Helen Keller shows what an expansion and mediation speech can bring to the child's anger and anxiety, as well as how it can be a mask, a fictionalization as much as a genuine expression, as perhaps in those individuals who do not possess it fully. At all events, these various modalities of speech, which are just so many ways of relating us to the universal, bind speech to a *modus vivendi*.

We have sought further confirmation of the fundamental role of speech in certain pathological disintegrations, drawing upon Kurt Goldstein's work, *Language and Language Disturbances*.[2] In earlier works Goldstein distinguished between an automatic language (an "external verbal knowledge") and language in the full sense (genuine denomination), which is related to a "categorical attitude." The question arises whether these early distinctions put signification into language *like a pilot in a boat*. In the 1948 work, however, these two orders are related so that there is no longer signification on the one hand and the "instrumentalities" of language on

2. New York: Grune and Stratton, 1948.

the other. In the long run, the instrumentalities of language only remain functional as long as the categorical attitude is intact and, inversely, the impairment of the instrumentalities compromises the grasp of signification. There is thus a sort of spirit of language, a spirit always freighted with language. For language is the system of differentiations through which the individual articulates his relation to the world. The conception of neurological pathology in terms of dedifferentiation and the Saussurian notion of the diacritical sign are interrelated and akin to Humboldt's idea of language as a "perspective on the world." There is also a reminiscence of Humboldt in Goldstein's analysis of the "internal form of language" (*innere Sprachform*), which, according to him, mobilizes the instrumentalities of language, either in the perception of the verbal chain or in elocution. The spirit becomes dependent upon the linguistic organism which it has created, into which it continues to breathe life, though the latter in turn communicates its own impulse as though it had its own source of life. The categorical attitude is not an act of pure spirit, but presupposes a live functioning of the "internal forms of language." Instead of being framed in Kantian terms, the categorical attitude is now anchored in articulated language. For articulated language is able to manipulate empty symbols; it not only brings a surplus of meaning to a given situation, as in a cry or gesture, but can itself evoke its own context and induce the mental framework which is its source; in other words, it is, in the full sense of the word, expression. "We may say that the development of the categorical attitude is a function of the degree of development of language toward eminently conventional forms in which, as we have said, the maximum of indeterminacy in the symbols yields the maximum determination of the object." [3] Although none of the authors mentions him, one can recognize in this immanent spirit of language the mediator which Saussure called speech.

Again, it is this same spirit of language that the writer encounters professionally. The act of writing, says Proust, is in a sense the opposite of speech and life because it opens us to others as they are at the same time that it closes us to ourselves. The writer's speech, on the contrary, itself creates an "allocutor" capable of understanding and imposes a private world upon him as something evident. But in doing so it only reactivates the original operation of language with the deliberate aim of acquiring and putting into circulation not just the statistical and common aspects of the world, but its very manner of touching and inserting itself into the individual's experience. It cannot therefore be content with the established and current significations. Just as the painter and the musician make use of objects, colors, and sounds in order to reveal the relations between the elements of the world in a living unity—

3. A. Ombredane, *L'Aphasie et l'élaboration de la pensée explicite* (Paris: Presses Universitaires de France, 1951), pp. 370–71.

for example, the metaphorical correspondences in a marine landscape—so the writer takes everyday language and makes it deliver the prelogical participation of landscapes, dwellings, localities, and gestures, of men among themselves and with us. In literature, ideas, as in music and painting, are not the "ideas of the intellect"; they are never quite detached from what the author sees; they are transparent, as unchallengeable as persons, but not definable. What has been called Proust's Platonism is an attempt at an integral expression of the perceived or lived world. For this reason, the writer's work is a work of language rather than of "thought." His task is to produce a system of signs whose internal articulation reproduces the contours of experience; the reliefs and sweeping lines of these contours in turn generate a syntax in depth, a mode of composition and recital which breaks the mold of the world and everyday language and refashions it. This new speech takes shape in the writer unnoticed, during years of apparently idle living in which he despairs of the lack of literary ideas and "subjects"—until one day he yields to the weight of that *way of speaking* which has gradually been built up in him and he starts to say how he became a writer, creating a work from the story of the birth of that work. Thus literary speech expresses the world insofar as it has been given to someone to live it and at the same time it absorbs the world and poses itself as its proper goal. Proust was right, therefore, when he stressed that speech or writing could become a manner of living. He would have been wrong to think (which he did not) that this way of life more than any other could embrace and suffer everything. However, no one has better expressed the vicious circle or prodigy of speech, that to speak or to write is truly to *translate* an experience which, without the word that it inspires, would not become a text. "The book of unknown signs within me (signs in relief it seemed, for my attention, as it explored my unconscious in its search, struck against them, circled round them like a diver sounding) no one could help me read by any rule, for its reading consists in an act of creation in which no one can take our place and in which no one can collaborate." [4]

These descriptions of the inchoate, regressive, and sublimated forms of speech should enable us to study its relation in principle to instituted language and to clarify the nature of institution as the act of the birth of all possible speech. This will form the topic of another course. [5]

4. Marcel Proust, *A la recherche du temps perdu*, II, 23.
5. Probably a reference to the course on "Institution in Personal and Public History," chapter 5 below.

4 / Materials for a Theory of History

THE CONCEPT OF HISTORY must be disentangled from a number of confusions. It is often argued as though there were, on the one hand, a philosophy which ascribes to man values ascertainable outside of time, a consciousness unrestricted by any interest in actual events, and, on the other hand, those "philosophies of history" which discover in the flow of events an occult logic whose outcome we can only wait upon. We should then have to choose between the wisdom of an understanding which does not flatter itself upon discovering a meaning to history, but merely tries constantly to bend history toward our values, and a fanaticism that in the name of the secret of history gleefully overturns the most evident of our beliefs. But this is an artificial cleavage: there is no question of choosing between external events and the internal spirit of man, between history and the timeless. All the instances that one might care to oppose to history have their own history through which they communicate with history, although they have their own way of using time. Furthermore, nothing, not even a political movement, is enclosed in a moment of time and in this sense it is not *in* history, for the most passionate stances can have an inexhaustible bearing—like a monogram of the spirit in things.

The real problem is always hidden by traditional discussions of historical materialism. It does not matter so much to know that one is a "spiritualist" or a "materialist" in his approach to history as to know how one understands the spirit and the material of history. There are conceptions of the "spiritual" which so isolate it from human life that it is as inert as matter, and there can be a "historical materialism" which incorporates the whole of man in the economic and social struggle. History effects an exchange between all levels of activity so that none of them can be dignified with exclusive causality. The question is rather to know if this concatenation of the problems is an indication of the simultaneity of their resolution or whether this convergence and recuperation exists only in the process of interrogation.

The proper starting point is not from the alternatives of understanding and history or spirit and matter, but from those of history as an unknown god—the good or evil genius—and history as the milieu of life. History is a milieu of life if it can be said that there is, between theory and practice, between culture and man's labor, between epochs and individual lives, between planned actions and the time in which they mature, an affinity that is neither fortuitous nor grounded in an omnipotent logic. Historical action is invented and yet it responds so well to the problems of the time that it is understood and followed, so that, as Péguy said, it incorporates itself into the "public duration." It would be simply a retrospective illusion to project the historical act into the past which it transforms. But, similarly, it would be a *prospective illusion* to bring the present to a halt on the threshold of an empty future, as though each present did not prolong itself toward a horizon of the future, and as though the meaning of a period which is decided by human initiative were *nothing* before that. Historical invention works through a matrix of open and unfinished significations presented by the present. Like the touch of a sleepwalker, it touches in things only what they have in them that belongs to the future. If the historical talent of great men were only a technique for manipulating others, there would surely be those adventures in history which endure and are always part of its scenery, but history would lack those exemplary actions which constitute a step into the public duration and inscribe themselves in the human memory, whether they last a month, a year, or a century. There is no history where the course of events is a series of episodes without unity, or where it is a struggle already decided in the heaven of ideas. History is there where there is a logic *within* contingence, a reason *within* unreason, where there is a historical perception which, like perception in general, leaves in the background what cannot enter the foreground but seizes the lines of force as they are generated and actively leads their traces to a conclusion. This analogy should not be interpreted as a shameful organicism or finalism, but as a reference to the fact that all symbolic systems—perception, language, history—only become what they were although in order to do so they need to be taken up into human initiative.

This idea of history was not systematically developed in this course. We tried to outline it through the researches of such people as Max Weber and his pupil Georg Lukács (particularly in *Geschichte und Klassenbewusstsein,* Berlin, 1923), who confirm the necessity of a path between the philosophy of understanding and the dogmatic philosophies of history.

As a point of departure, Max Weber gives particular attention to the radical contingency and infinity of the historical fact. From a "Kantian" perspective, historical objectivity therefore appears simply as the correlative of the historian's theoretical operation. It cannot flatter itself with having exhausted the reality of *history which has passed.* For, being in principle always tentative, it can only illuminate one aspect of an event and is lacking in any methodical abstraction which would eliminate other aspects of the event; thus of itself it calls forth further analyses and points of view. Max Weber is led by this antithesis between reality and constructed objectivity to draw an absolute contrast between the attitude of knowledge, which is always provisional and conditional, and practice, where on the contrary we encounter reality and assume the infinite task of evaluating the event as it happens, taking a position without any possibility of reprieve and under condi-tions quite contrary to those presupposed by theoret-ical justification. In practice we inevitably find our-selves in conflict and our decisions both justifiable and unjustifiable. Weber leaves the two spheres of knowledge and practice juxtaposed without any re-lation, and within the latter the conflicting options of the ethic of responsibility and the ethic of faith. This attitude is a constant feature of his career. It makes out of history a sort of malefactor.

However, in his empirical studies Weber disre-gards these antitheses. He starts with the observa-tion that there is a profound analogy between the task of the historian who undertakes to understand events and that of the man of action when prepar-ing his decision. Knowledge is gained by putting ourselves in the position of those who have acted; it is action in the realm of the imagination. But action is an anticipation of knowledge; it makes us histori-ans of our own lives. With regard to the radical pluralism of options, even a "polytheistic" system establishes a hierarchy among its gods. Moreover, a persistent profession of polytheism would imply *a certain* image of historical reality. The conflicting options of the ethic of responsibility and the ethic of faith are not exclusive. For even pure faith chooses the moment to declare its sincerity and the calculation of consequences is often a veiled judgment of value. Weber concludes with the admission (*Politik als Beruf*)[1] that here we are dealing with abstract limits between which, for better or worse, we try to steer in our daily politics.

This presupposes or entails a re-examination of the concept of history. It must be that *what has happened* should not be a reality in principle inimical to knowledge. Whatever comes to pass, however unfathomable it may be, must not conceal any "positive irrationality." And so, indeed, in such analyses as his famous study of *The Protestant Ethic and the Spirit of Capitalism,* Weber penetrates the interior of the historical fact far beyond what his "Kantian" principles allowed him and goes beyond the theoretical construction in the direction of historical "comprehension." He undertakes to get at the fundamental "choice" in the Calvinist ethic and the "affinity" of that choice with those other choices in Western history which, in conjunction with it, made capitalist enterprise possible (namely, the establishment of science and technology, law, and the state). The notion of an "affinity of choices" (*Wahlverwandtschaft*) makes the event something other than a conjunction of circumstances but without it appearing as an imminent historical necessity. It is

1. Max Weber, "Politics as a Vocation," in *From Max Weber: Essays in Sociology,* trans. and ed. H. H. Gerth and C. Wright Mills (New York: Oxford University Press, 1958) —*Trans.*

as though it were only in contact with one another that these choices together were able finally to produce Western capitalism, without the essence of the system pre-existing their encounter. Pluralism, which formerly seemed to ban any attempt at a unified interpretation of history, on the contrary now attests the solidarity of the economic order, and those of politics, law, morals, or religion as soon as the economic order itself is treated as the choice of a relation between men and with the world and takes its place in the logic of choice. Even the metamorphosis of the past by the conception which succeeds it presupposes a sort of understanding in depth between the present and the past. Our views would not overturn the image of the past if they were not "interested" in it, if they didn't envisage the totality of man, if our age were content with itself, or unless the past and the present belonged to a single realm of culture, that is to say, the replies that man freely makes to a permanent questioning. Our contact with our age is an initiation into every age; man is a historian because he belongs to history and history is only the amplification of practice.

History is no longer a tête-à-tête between a Kantian understanding and a past in itself; understanding now discovers in its object its own origins. The methodical attitude of the "objective" historian itself becomes part of a more inclusive history and is a species of that "rationalization" which at other levels produces capitalist society and the state, in the modern sense. Thus there is in Weber the outlines of a phenomenology of historical choices which uncovers the intelligible matrices into which the infinite detail of facts is inserted. This phenomenology is quite different from Hegel's because the meaning which it discovers in historical facts is unstable and always threatened. Capitalism denatures the Calvinist ethic from which it arises and preserves only its external form or "shell," as Weber says. Historical experience is never absolutely conclusive because the question which moves it transforms itself along the way. As a reply to a question poorly posed, historical experience is itself equivocal. The "rationalization," the demystification of the world, comprises both gains and losses, for it is also a "disenchantment" and makes the order of the day, in Weber's phrase, a "petrified" humanity. And so the logic of choices is not necessarily extrapolated into a confirmable future in which the problem *treated* by Calvinism and capitalism would finally be *resolved*. The philosophy of history does not add the revelations of a universal history to the certitudes of the understanding. It is rather through an unending interrogation that all the ages together compose a single and universal history.

The interest of what has come to be an old book of Lukács' is that it attempts to push the comprehension of history further than Weber and thus to rejoin Marxian intuitions—providing an opportunity to examine the possibility of a historical dialectic free from any dogmatic tutelage, having become a genuine *concrete dialectic*.

Lukács takes the present as his point of departure in aiming at a view of the totality which is intended to appear only as a "totality of experience." Lukács resumes the Weberian intuition of capitalism as "rationalization," and he determines its species and animation by developing its pre-capitalist past and the post-capitalist future and by comprehending it as a process and not an immobile essence. In comparison with pre-capitalist civilizations, capitalism represents the very embodiment of society (*Vergesellschaftung der Gesellschaft*). In so-called primitive civilizations collective life is in part imaginary, for between those elements which are capable of an economic interpretation there subsist lacunae or interworlds, which are occupied by myth. Myth is not an ideology, that is to say, the veiling of an economic reality which has to be uncovered but has its proper function because these societies have not yet broken the "umbilical cord" which ties them to nature. It is this rupture which capitalist civilization is destined to consummate and thereby the integration of a social system which, demystified or disenchanted, is organized as a capitalist economy and thus into a single field of forces which from its own momentum opens itself to an interpretation of its unity which grasps it in its *truth*. Nevertheless, the integration of society is checked by an internal impediment: both in theory and in practice the system fails to master the life of the social collectivity. In order to escape a total judgment which it tends to induce, capitalism poses itself as the eternal structure of the social world instead of a transitory phase in the social dynamic and the movement toward an objective understanding, which had laid the basis for a social consciousness, hardens into objectivism and scientism. This phase of social science is only an aspect of the general process of *reification* which separates capitalist civilization from its human origins and endows commodities and the laws of exchange in a market economy with a categorical value. In the proletariat Lukács discovers the class that is able to bring this sketch of society to its completion. Being in reality the extreme degree and absolute refusal of "reification," it is in fact and in principle "at the heart of the social process" and finds itself in a position to create and sustain a society that would genuinely be a transparent society, internally undivided and classless. With power in the hands of the proletariat, a system of production would be achieved which would not be shackled by its own forms, and would in turn provide the conditions for genuine knowledge of society and the whole of history.

The new society would outgrow the polemical concepts which it used in the struggle and, for example, Lukács specifies that historical materialism would change its function and meaning. In other words, the parallelism between economics and history, which in the capitalist stage of history meant that history was to be explained in terms of economics, in post-capitalist society would mean the equally free development of unimpeded knowledge and production.

Despite the numerous questions raised by this analysis, we are interested in it only from a methodological standpoint inasmuch as it offers an image of philosophy, or the quest for truth, as the concentration of a meaning scattered through history or outlined in it. There is no question of a philosophical reconstruction of history in terms of those provisional and abstracted frames of reference of which Max Weber spoke, because what is involved is the explanation of the movement of history through the constitution within it of a class described as the "suppression of itself" (*Selbstaufhebung*) and the advent of the universal. Truth is not found in certain historical agents nor in the achievement of theoretical consciousness, but in the confrontation of the two, in their practice, and in their common life. So conceived, history is the genesis of truth and the "philosophy of history" is no longer a transcendental discipline but a coherent and total explication of the meaning of human development, which of its nature is essentially "philosophical." The circle of existence to which Weber gave a theoretical formula, in his remark that man is a historian because he is in history and because his practice is a call to knowledge and theory, reappears in Lukács in the form of a knowledge and practice which are solidary and open. Thus Hegelian rationalism is put in question, for it is only afterwards, once human invention has reintegrated them in the meaning of the totality, that the hazards of history can appear to be and are in fact rational without there being any place for the assumption of a hidden reason which orients them through the "ruse" of appearing in the guise of contingency. The logic of history imposes problems on the course of events and so long as they are not solved the contradictions accumulate and interact. But it does not of necessity impose any solution— the solution chosen by Lukács is only the incarnation of negativity in history, of the power of doubt and interrogation which Weber called "culture."

Can one continue to think that negativity remains identical once it has acquired a historical vehicle? It is all the more doubtful because Weber himself has renounced this position. Today, he emphasizes the opaqueness of social reality as a "second nature" and thus seems to postpone infinitely the limiting concept of transparent social relationships and therewith the categorical definition of history as the genesis of truth. This amounts to questioning the Marxist idea of a meaning which is imminent in history. This question should now be reopened.

5 / Institution in Personal and Public History

THE CONCEPT OF INSTITUTION may help us to find a solution to certain difficulties in the philosophy of consciousness. For consciousness there are only the objects which it has itself constituted. Even if it is granted that certain of the objects are "never completely" so (Husserl), they are at each moment the exact reflection of the activity and faculties of consciousness. There is nothing in the objects capable of throwing consciousness back toward other perspectives. There is no exchange, no interaction between consciousness and the object. When consciousness considers its own past, all that it knows is that for a long time there has been this other, mysteriously called me, but with whom I have nothing in common except an absolutely universal ipseity which I share just as much with every "other" of whom I can form a concept. My past has yielded to my present by means of a series of fragmentations.

Finally, when consciousness considers others, their existence only means the negation of itself; it does not know that they behold it, it only knows that it is beheld. Different times and diverse temporalities are incompossible and merely form a system of reciprocal exclusions.

If the subject were taken not as a constituting but an instituting subject, it might be understood that the subject does not exist instantaneously and that the other person does not exist simply as a negative of myself. What I have begun at certain decisive moments would exist neither far off in the past as an objective memory nor be present like a memory revived, but really between the two as the field of my becoming during that period. Likewise my relation to another person would not be reducible to a disjunction: an instituting subject could coexist with another because the one instituted is not the immediate reflection of the activity of the former and can be regained by himself or by others without involving anything like a total recreation. Thus the instituted subject exists between others and myself, between me and myself, like a hinge, the consequence and the guarantee of our belonging to a common world.

Thus what we understand by the concept of institution are those events in experience which endow it with durable dimensions, in relation to which a whole series of other experiences will acquire meaning, will form an intelligible series or a history—or again those events which sediment in me a meaning, not just as survivals or residues, but as the invitation to a sequel, the necessity of a future.

The concept of institution has been approached through four different levels of phenomena, of which the first three deal with personal or inter-subjective history and the last with public history.

There exists something comparable to institu-tion even at the animal level (the animal is impreg-nated by the living creatures which surround him at birth)—and even at the level of human functions which used to be considered purely "biological" (puberty reveals a conservation rhythm—the recall and transcendence of earlier events—relevant here is the oedipal conflict—which is characteristic of institution). However, in man the past is able not only to orient the future or to furnish the frame of reference for the problems of the adult person, but beyond that to give rise to a *search,* in the manner of Kafka, or to an indefinite elaboration: in this case conservation and transcendence are more profound, so that it becomes impossible to explain behavior in terms of its past, anymore than in terms of its future. The analysis of love in Proust reveals this "simultaneity," this crystallization upon each other of the past and the future, of subject and "object," of the positive and the negative. At first approxima-tion, sentiment is an illusion and its institution a habit, since it involves a transference of a way of loving learned elsewhere or in childhood. It is a kind of love which never holds for anything but an inte-rior image of the "object," and for such a love to be true and to really reach the other person it would be necessary that it had never been lived by anyone. However, once it has been recognized that pure love is impossible and that it would be a pure negation, it remains to establish that this negation is a fact, that this impossibility has happened. Thus Proust envisages a *via negativa* of love, manifest beyond any question in the experience of chagrin, despite the fact that the latter is the reality of separation and jealousy. At the highest point of alienation, jealousy becomes disinterestedness; it is quite impossible to pretend that a present love is nothing but a reverberation of the past. On the contrary, the past takes on the outline of a preparation or premeditation of a present that exceeds it in meaning although it recognizes itself in it.

The institution of a painter's work, or of a style in the history of painting, reveals the same subterranean logic. A painter learns to paint other than by imitating his predecessors. Each of his works announces those to follow—and makes it so that they cannot be the same. Everything hangs together, and yet he cannot say in which direction he is going. Likewise, in the history of painting, problems (such as that of perspective, for example) are rarely resolved directly. The search halts at an impasse, other inquiries seem to create a diversion, but the new thrust seems to enable the obstacle to be overcome from another direction. Thus, rather than a *problem,* there is an "interrogation" of painting, which lends a common significance to all its endeavors and binds them into a history, but never such that it can be anticipated conceptually.

Is all this true merely of the preobjective domain of personal life and art? Is there, in the development of knowledge, a manifest logic to which knowledge conforms? If there is such a truth, should not the truths be coordinated in a system which only gradually reveals itself, but whose entirety resides in itself outside of time? In order to be more agile and apparently more free, the development of knowledge manifests the same internal circulation between the past and present which has been observed in other institutions. The series of "idealizations" which reveals the whole number as a special case of a more essential number does not land us in an intelligible world from which it might be deduced; rather it resumes the evidence proper to the whole number, which remains understood. The historicity of knowledge is not an "apparent" characteristic of knowledge which would leave us free to define truth "in itself" analytically. Even in the order of exact knowledge what is held is a "structural" conception of truth (Wertheimer). Truth exists in the sense of a field common to the diverse enterprises of knowledge.

If theoretical consciousness, in its most assured forms, is not free from historicity, one might think that in return history would benefit from a *rapprochement* with theory and, with the preceding restrictions concerning the notion of system, allow itself to be dominated by thought. This would be to overlook that thought only has access to another historical horizon, to another "mental toolbox" (L. Febvre) through the self-criticism of its categories, through a lateral penetration and not by a sort of ubiquity in principle. There occurs a simultaneous decentering and recentering of the elements in our personal life, a movement by us toward the past and of the reanimated past toward us. Now this working of the past against the present does not culminate in a closed universal history or a complete system of all the possible human combinations with respect to such an institution as, for example, kinship. Rather, it produces a table of diverse, complex probabilities, always bound to local circumstances, weighted with a coefficient of facticity, and such that we can never say of one that it is more true than another, although we can say that one is more false, more artificial, and less open to a future in turn less rich.

These fragmentary analyses are intended as a revision of Hegelianism, which is the discovery of phenomenology, of the living, real and original relation between the elements of the world. But Hegelianism situates this relation in the past in order to subordinate it to the systematic vision of the philosopher. Now phenomenology is either nothing but an introduction to absolute knowledge, which remains a stranger to the adventures of experience, or phenomenology dwells entirely within philosophy; it cannot conclude with the predialectical formula that "being exists" and it has to take into account the mediation of being. It is this development of phenomenology into a metaphysics of history that we wished to outline here.

6 / The Problem of Passivity: Sleep, the Unconscious, Memory

How CAN WE IMAGINE that there is a subject which never encounters obstacles? If the subject has created the obstacles itself, then they are not obstacles. But if they really do offer resistance to the subject, then we are brought back to the difficulties of a philosophy which incorporates the subject in a cosmic order and treats the operation of spirit as a particular case of natural finality.

Every theory of perception runs into this problem, and thus an explication of perceptual experience should oblige us to become acquainted with a kind of being over which the subject is not sovereign and yet not enclosed within it.

In this course we have attempted to develop an ontology of the perceived world going beyond sensible nature. Whether we are trying to understand how consciousness can sleep, how it can be inspired by a past which it has apparently lost, or finally how

it can open up again to that past, it is possible to
speak of passivity only on the condition that "to be
conscious" does not mean "to give a meaning,"
which one projects onto an ungraspable object of
knowledge, but to realize a certain distance, a certain variation in a field of existence already instituted, which is always behind us and whose weight,
like that of an object in flight, only intervenes in the
actions by which we transform it. For man, to live is
not simply to be constantly conferring meaning
upon things but to continue a vortex of experience
which was set up at our birth, at the point of contact
between the "outside" and he who is called to live it.

Despite the words, sleep is not an act, the operation, the thought, or the consciousness of sleeping;
sleep is a modality of perceptual activity—more precisely, it is the provisional involution or differentiation of the latter. Sleep is the return to the inarticu-
lated, the resort to a global or prepersonal relation
to the world—which is not really absent but is,
rather, distant—in which our place is marked by the
body with which a minimum of contact is maintained that makes it possible to wake up. A philosophy of consciousness translates—and distorts—this
relation by postulating that sleep consists in being
absent from the real world or being present in an
imaginary world without any consistency, which is
to explain the negative in terms of the positive in
the absence of any criteria or controls. The negation
of the world in sleep is equally a way of upholding
it, and thus sleeping consciousness is not a recess of

pure nothingness: it is cluttered with the debris of the past and present; it plays among it.

A dream is not simply a variety of conscious imagination as it operates in waking states, namely, as a pure power of envisaging anything at all in any symbol whatsoever. If a dream were just this unlimited caprice, surrendering consciousness to its essential folly, which comes from having no substance and of becoming immediately what it invents or thinks it is, then it is difficult to see how consciousness once asleep could ever awaken, how it could ever take seriously the conditions in which awakening is an affirmation of reality, or how our dreams could have the sort of weight they have for us, which they owe to their relation with our past. The distinction between the real and the oneiric cannot be identical with the simple distinction between consciousness filled by meaning and consciousness given up to its own void. The two modalities impinge upon one another. Our waking relations with objects and others especially have an oneiric character as a matter of principle: others are present to us in the way that dreams are, the way myths are, and this is enough to question the cleavage between the real and the imaginary.

The discussion of dreams already raises the problem of the unconscious, the refuge of the subject in dream, of that which dreams in us, of the inexhaustible, indestructible fund from which our dreams are drawn. Freud has been rightly criticized for having introduced under the name of the unconscious a second thinking subject whose creations are simply received by the first, and he himself has admitted that this "demonology" was only a "misbegotten psychological conception." But discussion of the Freudian unconscious usually leads to a monopoly of consciousness: the unconscious is reduced to what we decide not to assume, and, since this decision presupposes that we are in contact with the repressed, the unconscious proves to be nothing more than a particular instance of bad faith, a hesitation of imaginative freedom. Such a view loses sight of what was Freud's most interesting insight —not the idea of a second "I think" which could know what we do not know about ourselves—but the idea of a symbolism which is primordial, originary, the idea of a "non-conventional thought" (Politzer) enclosed in a "world for us," which is the source of dreams and more generally of the elaboration of our life. To dream is not to translate a latent content, which is clear to itself (or to the second thinking subject), into the equally clear but deceiving language of manifest content. That would not be its "adequate" expression from the standpoint of awakened thought, without for that reason being its deliberate concealment. For the language of manifest content is *valid for* the latent content in virtue of certain equivalences, certain modes of projection called forth by the primordial symbolism and the structure of oneiric consciousness. In Freud's *Science of Dreams* there is a complete description of oneiric consciousness—the consciousness which ig-

nores the *no,* which only says *yes* tacitly, producing
for the analyst the responses he was expecting from
it, being incapable of speech, calculation and real
thoughts, and thus reduced to the subject's ancient
elaborations, so that our dreams are not circumscribed the moment we dream them, but import *en
bloc* into our present whole fragments of our previous duration. What these descriptions mean is
that the unconscious is a perceiving consciousness
and that it operates as such through a logic of implication or promiscuity, follows closer and closer a
path whose slope it cannot see clearly, and envisages objects and creatures through the negative that
it withholds, which suffices to regulate its steps
without enabling it to name them "by their name."
Like the dream, delirium is full of immanent truths
and moves through a network of relations equivalent to true relations of which it lacks possession yet
takes into account. Freud's contribution is not to
have revealed quite another reality beneath appearances, but that the analysis of given behavior always discovers several layers of signification, each
with its own truth, and that the plurality of possible
interpretations is the discursive expression of a
mixed life in which every choice always has several
meanings, it being impossible to say which of them
is the only true one.

The problem of memory remains a dead end as
long as one hesitates between the conceptions of
memory as conservation and memory as construction. It is always possible to show that conscious-

ness only finds in its "representations" what it has put into them, and thus that memory is construction —and that nevertheless another memory behind the latter is needed to measure the value of its creations, in other words, a past given gratuitously and in a way quite opposite to the operation of memory as construction. Only if we abandon the description of the problem in terms of "representation" can we reconcile the immanence and transcendence of the past, the activity and passivity of memory. Instead of a "representation" (*Vorstellung*), we might begin by viewing the present as a certain unique position of the index of being-in-the-world, and our relations with the present when the present slips into the past, like our relations with our surroundings, might be attributed to a postural schema which unfolds and shapes a series of positions and temporal possibilities, so that the body could be regarded as that which answers each time to the question "Where am I and what time is it?" Then there would be no question of any alternative between conservation and construction; memory would not be the opposite of forgetfulness, and it might be seen that true memory is to be found at the intersection of the two, at the moment where memory forgotten and kept by forgetfulness returns. It might then be clear that forgetfulness and memory recalled are two modes of our oblique relation with a past that is present to us only through the determinate void that it leaves in us.

These phenomenological descriptions are always

somewhat misleading because they limit themselves to unraveling the negative in the positive and the positive in the negative. Reflection seems to demand supplementary clarification. Description will only have its full import when one begins to question oneself about the foundations of this need itself and gives reasons why in principle the relations between the positive and the negative present themselves as they do, which is to lay the foundations of a dialectical philosophy.

7 / Dialectical Philosophy

THE VERY TITLE OF THIS COURSE assumes the existence of a mode of thinking which, despite their differences, is common to so-called "dialectical" philosophers. There is no question of justifying this idea by the methods of inductive history. However, neither is it a matter of *replacing* the conclusions of history (supposing history could ever be conclusive) with a model. We propose simply to circumscribe a mode of thought and to sketch certain themes, which are as relevant today as they were yesterday. The various philosophies from the past are introduced—particularly in Monday's course [1]—solely to lend a voice to this schema. This analysis is intended to reclaim philosophy's right simply to reflect upon its past, to rediscover itself within it. In its place this is a legitimate exercise

1. "Texts and Commentaries on the Dialectic," pp. 60–61 below.—*Trans.*

within the history of philosophy. It is all the more so even if it limits itself to what past philosophies *could have meant,* taking into account their historical context, their internal structure, and their explicit problems.

Dialectical thought has been defined as follows:

[1] DIALECTIC OF CONTRADICTORIES

This means a dialectic which does not admit between contradictory terms either the relativist reconciliation or that identification through equivocation played upon by the "bad dialectic." If each of the opposed terms is nothing but the absence or the impossibility of the other, then they call for each other to the degree that they exclude one another and so pass in continual succession before a mind which is never able to posit them. An effective contradiction exists only where the relation between the positive and the negative is not one of alternation, but where the negation of the negation is capable of exercising its function against itself as an abstract or immediate negation and so founding contradiction while founding its transcendence. The Hegelian notion of the *negation of the negation* is not a solution of despair, nor is it a verbal artifice to escape from embarrassment. It is the formula of every operative contradiction and by leaving it aside one abandons dialectical thought itself, which is the fecundity of contradiction. The notion of a labor of the negative, as a negation which neither exhausts itself in the exclusion of the positive nor, when confronted with it, exhausts itself in conjuring up a term which annuls it, but instead reconstructs the positive beyond its limitations, destroying it and preserving it, is not a gradual perfecting or sclerosis of dialectical thought: it is its primordial resort (moreover, it is not astonishing to find it intimated in Plato where he calls the "same" the "other than the other"). We have related the notion of negation to the modern notion of *transcendence,* that is to say, to a being which is in principle at a distance, in regard to which distance is a bond but with which there can be no question of coincidence. Here, as in the other case, the relation of self to self passes through the external, the immediate demands mediation, or, again, mediation exists through the self.

[2] "Subjective" Dialectic

Dialectical thought developed after the philosophy of reflection and in a sense is its adversary since it conceives its own beginning as a problem, whereas the philosophy of reflection reduces the unreflected, as a simple absence, to the meaning which reflection thereafter discovers in it. However, one can say that the dialectic is "subjective" reflection in the sense understood by Kierkegaard or Heidegger, namely, that it does not make being rest upon itself but makes it appear before someone as the response to an interrogation. It is not simply a question, as someone has said, of "relativizing subject and object." Like all "relativist" thought this remark limits itself to handling the common life of the opposed terms by reducing contradiction to a difference in relations. But it will not suffice to say vaguely that the object is subjectivity in a certain relation and subjectivity is object in another relation. It is by means of what is most negative within subjectivity that it needs a world and by means of what is most positive within it that being needs non-being in order to circumscribe and delimit being. Thus dialectical thought invites us to revise the ordinary notions of subject and object.

[3] CIRCULAR DIALECTIC

Because dialectical thought is unwilling to sacrifice to the other either reflection or the unreflected it sees itself as the simultaneous development and destruction of that which preceded it and thus its conclusions retain the whole progression by which they were achieved. In truth, the dialectical conclusion is only the integration of the preceding advances. The dialectician is thus a perpetual beginner. That is to say, the circularity of dialectical thought is not that of a reflection which has made all the rounds and found nothing new to reflect upon. On the contrary, truth would cease to be an operative truth if it were to separate itself from its own development, or to forget it or really to put it in the past; and so everything has always to be re-thought in the dialectic. It is therefore no accident that in the nineteenth century the dialectic was "applied" to history and that in this field the dialectic simply comes into its own. For it is essential to it to realize itself only gradually, to move on and never express itself, as Hegel says, "in a single proposition." Already in Plato, as is shown by the famous "parricide" in the *Parmenides,* the notion of genesis or historical filiation is included among those negations which interiorize and conserve and is regarded as a principal example of a dialectical relation. Finally, although here again Hegel only provided the formula, the dialectic has always been conceived as an *experience* of thought, in other words, a journey in the course of which it learns, even though what it learns was already there, "in itself," before reflection which is only its passage to being for itself.

Understood in this way, dialectical thought is an uneasy equilibrium. As negative thought, it contains an element of transcendence and is unable to limit itself to the relation of multiplicity but is open, as Plato said, to an ἐπέκεινα τῆς οὐσίας. But, furthermore, this transcendence of being, whose source remains fixed, unlike the One of the First Hypothesis in the *Parmenides,* can be neither thought nor being and always appears only through a plural participation. There is therefore a dialectical absolute solely for the sake of maintaining the position and contours of the multiple and to oppose the absolutization of relations. It is "fluidified" in them and it is immanent to experience. This is a position which is unstable by definition and is always threatened either by positivist or negativist thought.

In the latter part of the course, we propose to study some of these deviations. In Hegel we examined the transition of the dialectic to speculation, of the "negatively rational" to the "positively rational," which finally transforms the dialectic into a system. And in the definition of the absolute we saw the balance swing in favor of the subject which thus gives an ontological priority to "interiority" and in particular dispossesses nature of its own concept, making exteriority a "feebleness of nature." All the same, the critique of system and speculation in Hegel's successors does not constitute a genuine return to dialectical inspiration. In Kierkegaard, the polemic against "objective" and "world historical" thought is sane in itself and might have initiated a concrete dialectic. But it ends in an attack on mediation, which is to say dialectical thought itself, and with an endorsement, under the singular name of "decision" or "choice," of the task of distinction between contradictories, a faith determined by its ignorance, a joy defined by its suffering, a sort of "religious atheism." In Marx at the time of the 1844 Manuscript,[2] alongside a conception of history as

2. Karl Marx, *Economic and Philosophical Manuscripts of 1844*, ed. D. Struik, trans. M. Milligan (New York: International Publishers, n.d.).—*Trans.*

man's "act of birth" and as negativity, which he
defends against Feuerbach, we found a naturalist
philosophy which localizes the dialectic in the pre-
paratory phase of human "prehistory" and assumes
as its horizon, beyond communism, as the "negation
of the negation," the wholly positive life of man as a
"natural" or "objective" being which is the resolution
of the enigma of history. The latter philosophy is
definitely predominant in *Capital* (that is why Marx
could there define the dialectic as "the positive intelligence of things as they exist") and much more so
among Marxists. Among our contemporaries it is
again "negativist" thought which is dominant and
curiously colors their neo-Marxism. In Sartre there
can be no dialectic between the being which is
wholly positive and nothingness which "is not."
What takes its place is a sort of sacrifice of nothingness which devotes itself entirely to the manifestation of being and negates absolutely the absolute
negation that it is itself. Being at once master and
servant, negation and negated, the negative is equivocal in principle: its loyalty is a refusal, its refusal a
loyalty. In the order of being to which the negative
is a stranger, it is unable to find a criterion for its
choices. For, in founding a choice, a criterion would
subject negation to conditions and there are no conditions which guarantee and limit the relation of
being to nothingness. This relation is, so to speak,
total or null; it is total because nothingness is not
and it is not nothing because it demands totality.

Sartre's is a philosophy which manifests, more than any other has done, the crisis, the essential difficulty, and the task of the dialectic.

[4] TEXTS AND COMMENTARIES
ON THE DIALECTIC

This course was planned as a free commentary upon texts chosen within as well as outside dialectical philosophy for the light that they throw upon dialectical thought.

Zeno's arguments have been studied as a sort of test of dialectical thought by each generation of philosophers who have discussed them. At first considered (and by Bergson still) as *sophisms* to which a direct intuition must do justice, they were finally recognized as paradoxes characteristic of the mathematical relations between the finite and the infinite (A. Koyré). The legend of Zeno illustrates the transition of a thought which denounces logical scandals in the name of an ideal of identity to a thought which on the contrary welcomes contradiction as the movement of being, a transition from a garrulous and "ventriloquist" dialectic to the real dialectic.

Plato's *Parmenides*, as well as the *Theaetetus* and the *Sophist,* have been studied as examples of a thought which is neither ascendant nor descendant, which, so to speak, keeps its place. This served as an opportunity to discuss recent interpretations of dualism and decadence in Plato.

We then went on to note traces of the dialectic in authors who make no profession of it but harbor it unwittingly or even against their will. Such is the case with Montaigne, in whom it is, above all, the description of the paradoxes of the self and of the rare occasions, which constitute its wisdom, where we succeed in getting the whole of our being "to work in a single unity." Likewise Descartes, whose principle of the "order of reasons" offers us the least dialectical philosophy there ever was, but who found himself led to envisage an order which would not necessarily be linear and to suggest a *nexus rationum.* Finally, we saw the same in Pascal when he sketched a method of convergence and a conception of "order" which is quasi-perceptual, with digression and return to a center, which is to say, a dialectical theory of truth.

The transition from Kant's *Antinomy of Pure Reason* to Hegel's dialectic—described by M. Gueroult in his article of 1931 [3]—offered the occasion for a re-examination of the relation of philosophy to history and the history of philosophy as an exercise in dialectical thought.

3. Martial Gueroult, "Le Jugement de Hegel sur l'antithétique de la raison pure," *Revue de métaphysique et de morale,* 1931, pp. 413–39.—*Trans.*

8 / The Concept of Nature, I

IN TAKING THE CONCEPT OF NATURE as the
sole topic of this year's course, as well as next, we
may seem to be stressing an unreal problem. But the
neglect which has fallen upon the philosophy of
nature embraces also a certain conception of spirit,
history and man, namely, the assumption of making
them appear as pure negativity. By contrast, in returning to the philosophy of nature, we only seem to
be looking away from these fundamental problems;
in fact, we are trying to lay the ground for a solution
to them which is not *immaterialist*. Naturalism
apart, an ontology which leaves nature in silence
shuts itself in the incorporeal and for this very reason gives a fantastic image of man, spirit and history. If we have stressed the problem of nature, it is
from the double conviction that it cannot by itself
solve the ontological problem but that neither is it a

subordinate or secondary element in any such solution.

At first sight it is astounding that Marxist philosophers have given so little attention to this problem, which should be their special concern. The concept of nature makes only brief and fleeting appearances in their works. It appears there only to attest that we are not in the in-itself, in an opaque being, a pure object. Yet what do we know about nature which allows us to assign it this ontological role? The question is not raised. The certitude of being in principle in the "objective" authorizes great inattention to its implications and numerous abstract constructions with respect to our knowledge of nature and matter. This poor dialectic has its origins perhaps in Marx himself. In the *Economic and Philosophic Manuscripts, 1844* nature is described on the one hand as a state of equilibrium existing in its own right—the stable being which will again close in upon human history at its end—and on the other hand as that which human history negates and transforms. Instead of being mastered or transcended, these two conceptions are simply juxtaposed, and finally forced to mix in the absolute of "objective activity" (*Theses on Feuerbach*): Thus it is possible that Marx's own philosophy presupposes a quite objectivist concept of nature, in order at times to affirm, and at others to negate nature. The result is always the same; even when a Marxist philosopher (G. Lukács) admits that Marxism cannot simply endorse Feuerbach's naturalism against Hegel's idealism, he nevertheless does not risk describing the third position, the true *medium* of the dialectic, but proceeds without further specification to a profession of "materialism." [1] With all the more reason, everyone avoids any confrontation between Engels' conception of nature and that which we have come to know in the last fifty years. The most famous of all philosophies of history rests upon a concept which has never been elucidated and which may be mythical. As a pure object, or being in itself, which contains everything that exists and yet is not to be found in human experience since from the very beginning man shapes and transforms it, nature in the Marxist philosophy of history is everywhere and nowhere, like a visitation. In trying to elucidate this problem, we are threfore not so far from history.

In truth, as soon as one probes into it a little, one encounters an enigma in which the subject, spirit, history and the whole of philosophy are involved. For nature is not simply the object, the accessory of consciousness in its tête-à-tête with knowledge. It is an object from which we have arisen, in which our beginnings have been posited little by little until the very moment of tying themselves to an existence which they continue to sustain and aliment. Whether in the case of the individual event of birth, or the birth of institutions and societies, the originary relation between man and being is not that of the for-itself to the in-itself, for this relation occurs in each man capable of perception. However surcharged with historical significations man's perception may be, it borrows from the primordial at least its manner of presenting the object and its ambiguous evidence. Nature, says Lucien Herr in a comment upon Hegel, "is there from the first day." It presents itself always as already there before us, and yet as new before our gaze. Reflexive thought is disoriented by this implication of the immemorial in the present, the appeal from the past to the most recent present. For reflexive thought each fragment of space exists on its own account and they can only coexist under its gaze and through its activity; each moment of the world ceases to exist when it ceases to be present and is only held in past being by reflexive thought. If it were possible to abolish in thought all individual consciousness there would remain only a flash of instantaneous being, extinguished no sooner than it has appeared. The phantom and tenacious existence of the past is converted into a posited being, which may be clear or confused, empty or full, but in any case is the exact correlative of our acts of knowing. All that is to be found at the limits of the spirit is *mens momentanea seu recordiatione carens*, that is to say, ultimately, nothing. If we are not to be resigned to saying that a world from which consciousness is cut off is nothing at all, then in some way we must recognize that primordial being which is not yet the subject-being nor the object-being and which in every respect baffles reflection. From this primordial being to us, there is no derivation, nor any break; it has neither the tight construction of the mechanism nor the transparency of a whole which precedes its parts. We can neither conceive of primordial being engendering itself, which would make it infinite, nor think of it being engendered by another, which would reduce it to the condition of a product and a dead result. As Schelling has remarked, there is in nature something which makes it such that it would impose itself upon God himself as an independent condition of his operation. Such is our problem.

Before trying to solve this problem, it was necessary to rediscover it in different traditions of thought. We have decided to begin, in this year's course, with a survey of the historical elements in our concept of nature. It is only following this that we begin to seek in the development of knowledge the symptoms of a new conception of nature. This task could only be undertaken this year with respect to physical nature. Next year we shall continue with the examination of the conception of life and culture to be found in contemporary research. Once this is done, we shall be in a position to ascertain the philosophical signification of the concept of nature.

[1] ELEMENTS OF OUR CONCEPT OF NATURE

1.

Since our aim is not to construct a history of the concept of nature, the pre-Cartesian conceptions of nature as a destiny or total dynamic of which man is a part have not been studied in their own right. It seemed preferable to take as a reference-point a "Cartesian" conception which, rightly or wrongly, still overhangs contemporary ideas about nature— which is likely to raise pre-Cartesian themes that remain alive long after Descartes.

2. *The Cartesian Idea of Nature*

Descartes admits that, even if God had created our world all at once with the structure that it has, the immanent play of the laws of nature would have imposed themselves upon Him and the same act since these laws stem of necessity from the attributes of finite being. This implies the reduction of the facticity of nature to its bare existence. Thus, the world might not have existed, had God not decided to create it; it therefore arose from a "before" in which nothing or no preponderant possibility prefigured it or called it into existence. But, once the world has arisen, it is necessitated to be such as we see it; it is what it is without hesitation, without error, without weakness; its reality contains no fault or fissure. The alternative of the world's nonexistence, which remains possible if we take God's view of things, in no way deprives it of its solidity. On the contrary, this alternative acknowledges the world's solidity because it makes it understood that, if the world were not such as we see it, it would not exist at all. God's being is defined by the same dilemma: to say that he is the cause of himself is to try to imagine that which is nothing and to maintain that, on this ground, one sees the emergence of a being who takes off and produces himself. The hypothesis of the Nothing, which had its truth with respect to the world, is in the latter case purely verbal: there has never been any possibility that God does not exist. It is however a hypothesis at the horizon of Descartes' thought: "cause of itself" would be meaningless if one were not to evoke for a moment, even fictionally, a God *effect,* which, like every effect, needs to be sustained by its cause and could not exist without it. Human beings are not able to think that which is nothing, they are surrounded by an infinite plenitude; when they set about thinking, the die is already cast: to think, it is necessary to be. Nevertheless, thought only recognizes itself at the highest point of doubt, in the moment where thought of its own accord denies everything that is. In the same manner, that which is cause of itself is only found through the dependence of all existing things, and the power with which it sustains its own existence is exactly proportionate to the hesitation which it ends.

Such is the ontological complex in which we find

the Cartesian concept of nature. It obliges every being, under pain of being nothing, to exist completely without hiatus, and with no hidden possibilities. There is to be nothing occult or enveloped in nature any more. Nature must be a mechanism and one should be able in principle to derive the form of this world from laws which are themselves the expression of the internal force of infinite production. In accordance with a distinction drawn long before Descartes but reinvigorated by his reflections, what we call nature is a *naturata,* a pure product, composed of absolutely external parts, completely existent and clearly combined—an "empty shell," as Hegel would say. Everything internal is handed over to God's side, the pure *naturans.* Both historically and philosophically our idea of natural being *qua* object in itself, which is what it is because it cannot be another thing, derives from the idea of an unlimited being, infinite or *causa sui,* and this in turn comes from the alternation between being and nothing. The Cartesian conception of nature will outlive this ontology, enduring as the common stock of scientists who continue to struggle to bring their own achievements within its jurisdiction until the quite un-Cartesian developments in contemporary science open up for them a different ontology.

Yet, even without going beyond Descartes' writings, one might have recognized the limitations of his ontology. For the concept of nature that we have referred to is in fact that which reveals to us its essence as evident, nature according to the *lumen naturale*. But, by maintaining the contingency of the act of creation, Descartes upheld the facticity of nature and thus legitimated another perspective on this existent nature than that of pure understanding. To this nature we have an access, not only through it, but through the vital relation that we have with a privileged part of nature: namely, our body, through the "natural inclination" whose lessons cannot coincide with those of pure understanding. It is life which validly comprehends the life of the human composite. But how can we leave the definition of being and truth to pure understanding if it is not grounded so as to know the existent world? Moreover, if we take into account the definition of space, for example, the space of our body with which we are united substantially, how can we maintain the definition of the extended object given to the understanding? Descartes' hesitations in the theory of the human body are witness to this difficulty. His position seems to be that for us the experience of existence is irreducible to the view of it in pure understanding, yet experience cannot teach us anything which might be contrary to understanding, and is not in itself—that is to say, for God—incompatible with understanding and his will: if nature exists only through the decision—and the continuing decision—of God, then it does not "hold" in time (nor for that matter in space) by necessity of its own fundamental laws. Nature as event or an ensemble of events remains different from nature as object, or an ensemble of objects, as does God conceived as the free creator of the world and God as the source of a causality from which derives an eminently finitized world.

3. Kantian Humanism and Nature

Kantianism abandons the derivation of natural being as the only possible manifestation of infinite being—but not in order to acknowledge it as brute being and to undertake its study. Such a study is declined in the *Critique of Pure Reason* by defining nature as "the sum of meaningful objects" (*Inbegriff der Gegenstände der Sinne*) coordinated under the *Naturbegriffe* of the human understanding. We can only speak of a nature that is nature for us; in this regard nature remains the object which Descartes had in mind, it is an object constructed by us.

However, Kant goes beyond this anthropological philosophy. The organism, in which every event is cause and effect of all the others, and in this sense cause of itself, raises the problem of an auto-production of the whole, or, more precisely, of a totality which, in contrast with human technique, works upon materials which are its very own and, so to speak, emanates from them. It seems that within an entity that is in the world one encounters a mode of liaison which is not the connection of external causality, that is, an "interior" unlike the interior of consciousness, and thus nature must be something other than an object. We need not wait, says Kant, for another Newton to help us understand by means of causal relations what a blade of grass is. How are we to ground these natural totalities? Are we to say that we must uphold in juxtaposition, as two aspects of human consciousness, both the order of causal explanation and the order of totality? Would we then hold that when localized in phenomena (with every reservation with respect to the things in themselves) these two modes of apprehension are equally legitimate and compatible? But the retreat to the human order of phenomena evokes by definition an order of things themselves in which diverse human perspectives are impossible, since all of them together are real. In order for causal explanation and the perception of the totality to be in principle equally legitimate, it is not sufficient to claim that both causality and totality are as dogma equally false. Both have to be considered true of objects and false only when held in exclusion of one another. The idea of a discursive understanding with the authority to order our experience, though confined to this task, implies at least the idea of a "non-discursive understanding" that would ground simultaneously the possibility of causal explication and the perception of totality. The philosophy of human representation is not false, it is superficial. It assumes a reconciliation of thesis and antithesis for which man is the theater but not the agent.

In the last analysis, Kant does not take this path, which was taken later by Romantic philosophy. Although he anticipated Schelling in his description of the enigma of an organic totality, of a natural production in which both form and materials have a common origin and thereby controvert any analogy with human technique, Kant definitely considers the "natural end" (*Naturzweck*) as merely an anthropological term, though legitimate enough. Reflections upon totality are inevitable in every human subject, since they express the pleasure we experience in establishing a spontaneous accord between the contingency of what exists and the legislation of the understanding. They in no way designate anything constitutive of natural being, but are simply the happy encounter of our faculties. Nature, as a sum of "meaningful objects," is defined in terms of the *Naturbegriffe* of Newtonian physics. We think about it much more in its own way, but these are only reflections of ours. If we wished to realize them as properties of the thing itself we should be prevented by the manifest failures of teleology. The consideration of nature from this standpoint would yield at best a "demonology." It is in the "concept of freedom" only and consequently in consciousness and man that the conformity of the elements to a concept takes on a real sense, so that the teleology of nature is a reflection of "noumenal man." The truth of teleology is the consciousness of freedom. Man is the only goal of nature, not because nature prepares him and creates him, but because man retroactively confers upon nature an air of finality by positing its autonomy.

The reappearance of Kantianism in the nineteenth century represents the victory of this anthropological philosophy over the philosophy of nature that Kant had envisaged and his successors had wished to develop. Léon Braunschvicg thought he could salvage the best in Kant by effacing the *a priori* structure of the understanding and the facticity of experience which was the motive in Kant for the ideal of an intuitive understanding. He treated the radical originality of natural being as an enigma. But the remedy only aggravates the ill. If, as Braunschvicg says, we no longer have the right to speak of an architectonic of nature, if the concepts of the understanding share in the contingency of experience and are always weighted by a "coefficient of facticity" which ties them to specific structures of the world, should our laws have no meaning except on the supposition of certain synchronisms of which they are not the source but merely an expression, and finally if there is, as the Stoics foresaw, a brute unity through which the universe "holds" and of which the unity of human understanding is the expression rather than the internal condition, then the being of nature is decidedly not its object-being and there reappears the problem of a philosophy of nature.

4. *Essays on the Philosophy of Nature*

The Cartesian conception of necessary being was overtly questioned by Schelling. To him, as for Kant, it was "the abyss of human reason." Necessary being could not be primary unless it was able to put itself in question. But, if it does so and raises, as Kant says, the question "Where am I?" it disqualifies itself as the primary being. Reflection cannot closet itself and withdraw into the idea of necessary being. But, whereas Kant abandons the idea as unknowable and mistaken (eventually to fall into a metaphysic of the subject), Schelling considers the "abyss" itself to be an ultimate reality and defines the absolute as that which exists without reason (*grundlos*), as the "over-being" who sustains the "grand fact of the world." Just as the absolute is no longer its own cause, or the absolute antithesis of nothingness, so nature no longer possesses the absolute positivity of "the only possible world." The *erste Natur* is an ambiguous principle, or, as he puts it, a "barbarous" principle which can be transcended, but will never be as though it had never existed, and can never be considered secondary even in relation to God. With all the more reason, can there be no question of explaining the enigma of natural production by our faculty of judgment or human reflection. "What Kant, at the end of his sober discourse, one day dreamed virtually," Schelling tries to think, or rather live (*leben*) and experience (*erleben*). What we have here is the "intellectual intuition," which is not an occult faculty, but perception as it is before it has been reduced to ideas; it is perception dormant within itself, in which all things are me because I am not yet the reflecting subject. At this level, light and air are not yet, as in Fichte, the milieu of vision and hearing, the means whereby rational creatures communicate, but "the symbols of an eternal and originary knowledge (*Urwissen*) inscribed in Nature." *Urwissen* is a bound and silent knowledge brought into being by man alone yet obliging us to say that man is the conscious development of the natural production, he who becomes nature is distancing himself from nature in order to learn about it. In principle (one cannot say as much for the poets and writers around him—nor even for the evil genius in Schelling which distracted him from his principles), nature in Schelling never gives rise to a second science or a gnosis which would objectivate and absurdly convert into a second causality the relations of existing nature as we glimpse them in the "ek-stasis" of intellectual intuition. There is only the effort to take account of the weight of the existing world, to make of nature something else than an "impotency" (Hegel) and an absence of the concept. Lukács [2] gives Schelling the honor of having introduced "the doctrine of the reflection (*Wiederspiegelung*) into transcendental philosophy," but regrets that he gave it an "idealist" and "mystic" twist. What Lukács considers irrational is doubtless the idea of an exchange between nature and consciousness within man, an internal relation between man and nature. It is clear, however, that the "doctrine of the reflection," or the mirror, leaves nature in the state of an *object* which we reflect, and that, if philosophy is to avoid immaterialism, it

2. Georg Lukács, *Die Zerstörung der Vernunft* (Berlin: Aufbau, 1955), p. 110.

must establish a more strict relation between man and nature than this looking-glass relation, since nature and consciousness can only truly communicate in us and through our incarnate being. And this is a relation which neither suppresses nor replaces the relation we have so richly with the human milieu of history; it merely invites us to conceive it in its turn as an effective contact, instead of construing it also as a "reflection" of a process which is historical in itself.

Bergson might seem to be far removed from what is best in Schelling. Bergson, unlike Schelling, does not seek the unreflected in a doubling of reflection ("intuition," as the young Hegel put it). He seems to take his stand wholly within the positive, and if he is dislodged from it in the course of his analysis it is as though despite himself and in complete unconsciousness of such a dialectic. Nevertheless there is enough substance in this criticism. To rediscover the dialectic despite oneself is perhaps a more sure way of taking it seriously than by starting from it, by knowing the formula or schema in advance and applying it everywhere in virtue of one of those *general* convictions that Spinoza referred to knowledge of the first order, without asking how it comes about that being is dialectical. Pure perception would be the thing itself. But no perception is pure; every effective perception makes itself before a "center of indetermination" and distance, this being the price that must be paid for the "discernment" of an articulated perception. This is not an unconscious shift in Bergson, but is clearly worked out. He does not conceive nature simply as the fascinating object of perceptual experience, but rather as a horizon from which we are already far away, a primordial lost undividedness, a unity which the contradictions of the developed universe negate and express in their own way, and in this sense it is correct to view Bergson in a line with Schelling. The analysis of the *élan vital* resumes the problem of organic nature in the rigorous terms in which it was raised in the *Critique of Judgment*. Like Kant and Schelling, Bergson wanted to describe an operation or a natural production which proceeds from the whole to the parts, but owes nothing to the premeditation of the concept and admits of no teleological explanation. That is the reason why the description of life in the first chapters of *Creative Evolution* is scrupulously honest. At the same time it hides nothing of its blindness, its hesitations, and, on many points, its failures. Moreover, the fact that Bergson speaks of a "simple act," that he assigns reality to the *élan* in advance of its effects as a cause which contains them pre-eminently, contradicts his own concrete analyses, and it is in these that we should seek the remedy. Bergson finds his way back to philosophy with the help of Spencer, though not without groping. Once on his own path, he ended by rediscovering the problems of being, of the positive and the negative, the possible and the actual, in which following generations have been expert from the crib. Perhaps it is not such a bad way. At least he owes it to this method to have made upon these abstract—that is to say, difficult *et faciles*—topics some remarks which bear the value of true research. Leaving aside his polemics against the ideas of disorder, nothingness, and possibility, we have tried to disentangle a worthwhile meaning of Bergsonian "positivism," which could not be defended strictly, nor was ever held strictly by Bergson himself. There is in Bergson an organic possibility and negativity which are the ingredients of being. His precept of returning to the evidence of the real should not be understood as a naive apology for verification, but as an allusion to the pre-existence of natural being, always already there, which is the proper concern of the philosophy of nature.

We have in the end retraced the path (as it is to be found in *Ideen* II) by which Husserl, having himself started from the most rigorous imperative of reflection, returned to the problem of nature. At first sight, nature appears as the correlative of the sciences of nature, as a sphere of "pure things" (*blosse Sachen*) without any value predicate which is posited before a purely theoretical subject. The theme of such an "objective," scientific thought is part of our intentional apparatus and arises as soon as we try to seize, objectivate, get hold of or grasp the true which we immediately confound with the in-itself. Husserl does not set out to destroy this notion, but to comprehend, that is to say, to reveal the intentional life which sustains, grounds, and constitutes it, and is the measure of its truth. In one sense, he says, objective being envelops everything, even the activity of consciousness upon which we would like to make it rest. For the philosopher who constitutes objective being is a man, he has a body, that body is in nature, and thereby philosophies themselves have their time and place, occur in the *universum realitatis*. There is a truth in naturalism. But that truth is not naturalism itself. For to acknowledge naturalism and the envelopment of consciousness in the universe of *blosse Sachen* as an occurrence, is precisely to posit the theoretical world to which they belong as primary, which is an extreme form of idealism. It is in fact to refuse to decipher the intentional references which run from the universe of *blosse Sachen,* or extended objects, to "pretheoretical objects," to the life of consciousness before science. The *blosse Sachen* are the secondary expression, actively constructed by the pure subject, of the primordial stratum of intuitive, perceived things. The problem is to bring into the open the motivations which lead from the one to the other.

Now, the intuitive properties of the perceived object depend upon those of the "body-subject" (*Subjektleib*) who experiences them. Consciousness of my body as the organ of a motor power, of an "I can," is presupposed in the perception of two objects at a distance from each other or even in the identification of two successive perceptions which I have of the same object. Moreover, my body is a "field of localization" in which sensations are set up.

In the act of exploring objects my right hand touches my left hand, touches it touching, and in this encounters "a feeling thing." Since there is a body-subject and since it is before this that objects exist, they are virtually incorporated in my flesh. But at the same time, our body projects us into a world of convincing objects, we come to believe in "pure objects," establishing the attitude of pure knowledge and forgetting the density of the corporeal "preconstitution" which sustains them.

It is not adequate, however, to evoke the functioning of my body in isolation in order to account for the pure Cartesian "in-itself." For the object perceived in the tissue of my corporeal experience would still be far from being a pure or true object: it is caught in this bodily experience like in a cocoon; there is no discernment at all of what is true in it or of what is only appearance with respect to my particular experience of it. I am far from understanding them all, since my body, which is always primary, is not yet objectivated. This happens only when I think of my body as a body among all other human bodies, and, for example, imagine my eyes as typical of those eyes that I can see. The solipsistic object of perception can only become a pure object on the condition that my body enters into systematic relations with other animate bodies. The experience which I have of my body as a field of localization of an experience and that which I have of other bodies in so far as they *behave* in front of me, come before one another and pass into one another. There are two perceptions which illumine one another and are fulfilled together. On the one hand, there is the perception which I have of my body as the seat of a "vision," of a "touch," and (since the senses flow together in it to their source in the impalpable consciousness from which they arise) of the perception of an *I think.* On the other hand, there is the perception which I have deep down of another "excitable," "sensible" body which (since all that does not occur without an *I think*) is the bearer of another *I think.* Thus I cannot be quite the incomparable monster of solipsism that I see myself. I strip from my experience whatever is bound to my corporeal singularities. I am in face of an object which is truly an object for everyone. The *blosse Sachen* are possible, but as the correlative of an ideal community of embodied subjects, of an intercorporeality.

This genesis of a *Kosmotheoros* which remained schematic in *Ideen* II (and was in any case contradicted at every point by the thesis of the irrelativity of consciousness) is described again by Husserl in his later writings. He sketches the description of those pre-objective beings which are the correlates of a community of perceiving bodies and stakes out its primordial history. Beneath Cartesian nature, which theoretical activity sooner or later constructs, there emerges an anterior stratum, which is never suppressed, and which demands justification once the development of knowledge reveals the gaps in Cartesian science. Husserl risks the description of the earth as the seat of pre-objective spatiality and temporality, as the homeland and historicity of bodily subjects who are not yet disengaged observers, as the ground of truth or the ark which carries into the future the seeds of knowledge and culture. Before being manifest and "objective," truth dwells in the secret order of embodied subjects. At the root and in the depths of Cartesian nature there is another nature, the domain of an "originary presence" (*Urpräsenz*) which, from the fact that it calls for the total response of a single embodied subject, is in principle present also to every other embodied subject.

Thus, a philosophy which seemed, more than any other, bent upon understanding natural being as the object and pure correlate of consciousness rediscovers through the very exercise of reflexive rigor a natural stratum in which the spirit is virtually buried in the concordant functioning of bodies within brute being. Cartesian nature had been conceived as self-sufficient, unable to lack being or not to be what it is, an inevitable being. At the end of the experience produced by this ontology European philosophy again confronts nature as an oriented and blind productivity. This does not represent a return to teleology. Properly speaking, teleology understood as the conformity of the event to a concept, shares the same fate as mechanism—these are both concepts of *artificialism*. Natural production has to be understood in some other way.

[2] CONTEMPORARY SCIENCE AND THE SIGNS OF A NEW CONCEPTION OF NATURE

In the last third of the year we began to look into contemporary science for the elements of a solution to the problem discussed above.

There is no need to justify the resort to science. Whatever one's conception of philosophy, its business is to elucidate experience, and science is a sector of our experience, admittedly subject to a very particular treatment by algorithm, yet in which in one way or another there is an encounter with being. This being so, it is not possible to reject science out of hand on the pretext that it works in terms of certain ontological prejudices. If these are indeed prejudices, then science itself, in its wanderings through being, will certainly have occasion to reject them. Being makes its path through science as through every individual life. From the interrogation of science philosophy stands to gain an encounter with certain articulations of being which otherwise it would find difficult to uncover.

Nevertheless one reservation must be made with regard to the philosophical use of scientific research: The philosopher, who lacks any professional competence in scientific techniques, should not pretend to intervene in the field, either in inductive research or to arbitrate for science. It is true that scientists' most general disputes do not arise over induction, as their most irreducible divergences show clearly enough. Here scientists try to express themselves at the level of language with the result that they cross over into philosophy. But this does not authorize philosophers to reserve to themselves the ultimate interpretation of scientific concepts. However, neither can they demand this interpretation from the scientists, who do not have it since they argue over it. Philosophers must find a way nicely between conceit and capitulation. This would involve asking science not what being is (science calculates *within being,* its constant procedure is to suppose the unknown known) but what being is certainly not; it would mean a scientific critique of the common notions outside of which philosophy cannot, on any hypothesis, establish itself. Science would contribute, as some physicists have said, "negative philosophical findings" (London and Bauer).

This is the spirit in which we have tried to show that science is always moving further away from the well-known definition of ontology given by Laplace. The critique of the classical concept of mechanics advanced in the past twenty-five years in wave mechanics could not possibly, whatever the outcome of the probabilistic interpretation, end in the restoration of Laplacean determinism. Here we have an intellectual experience which we have no right whatsoever to invoke in favor of a dogmatic acausality, but which alters the sense of causality. Even if one were, laboriously, to succeed by means of hidden parameters in putting its principles beyond reach—the very fact that they were hidden would reveal the occultism of dogmatic determinism. Certain philosophical descriptions of the perceived world may permit us to envisage what image of the world would positively express this self-criticism of determinism. For the perceived world is a world where there is discontinuity, where there is probability and generality, where each being is not constrained to a unique and fixed location, to an absolute density of being.

Similarly, the scientific critique of the forms of space and time in non-Euclidean geometry and relativity physics have taught us to break with the common notion of a space and time without reference to the observer's situation and enable us to give full ontological significance to certain descriptions of perceived space and time—to polymorphous space and time of which common sense and science retain only a few traces. Nor need the critique of absolute simultaneity in relativity physics necessarily lead to the paradoxes of the radical plurality of times—it might prepare the way for the recognition of a pre-objective temporality which is universal in its own way. Perceived time is, of course, solidary with the observer's point of view, but *by this fact* it constitutes the common dimension for all possible observers of one and the same nature. And this is so, not because we are constituted so as only to *attribute* to other observers an expanded or foreshortened time relative to our own—but rather the very contrary, in the sense that in its singularity our perceived time announces to us other singularities and other perceived times, with the same rights as ours, and in principle grounds the philosophical simultaneity of a community of observers. In place of Laplace's dogmatic objectivity, we glimpse an objectivity pledged upon the inherence of all thinking subjects in the same core of being which remains amorphous but with whose presence they experiment from within the situation to which they belong.

With all the more reason, a consideration of the sciences which Auguste Comte and Cournot called cosmological—that do not fix themselves upon constant relations but regard them as a means to reconstructing the development of the world, and, for example, of the solar system—would lead one to establish a regression of eternal ideologies in which nature is an object identical with itself and finally the emergence of a history—or, as Whitehead said, of a "process"—of nature. In the next course we shall pursue this analysis in the field of the life sciences.

9 / The Concept of Nature, II: Animality, the Human Body, Transition to Culture

IN ORDER TO SITUATE MORE CLEARLY the inquiry we are starting, we have decided to begin by going back to the relation between the problem of nature and the general problem of ontology. The study of nature is here an introduction to the definition of being, and in this respect one might just as well have started from man or God. In each case, it is a matter of knowing whether "being exists" is an analytic proposition, whether one can say quite simply that "being exists" and "nothingness does not exist." These questions, which could give rise to a whole philosophy, are raised in this instance from the standpoint of a certain sector of being, because it is perhaps a law of ontology always to proceed indirectly, and to lead up to being in general only through particular beings.

There are, for example, two senses of the word "nature" in Descartes (nature in the sense of "natu-

ral light" and nature in the sense of "natural inclination"). These two interpretations outline two ontologies (an ontology of the object and an ontology of
the existent) which Descartes attempted to reconcile in his later writings where he discovers the "being of God" (J. Laporte) beyond the possible and the
actual, beyond finality and causation, beyond will
and understanding in the "simple act," as E. Gil-
son and J. Laporte have both stressed. In Descartes as elsewhere, the notion of nature belongs to
an ontological complex, its avatars are the expression of a certain shift in the Cartesian ontology and
for this reason are of interest to us. It is possible
even that this shift in the Cartesian concept of nature is common to nearly all Western ontology. Can
we not find throughout our philosophy (and very
likely in our theology) a cycle or reverberation of a
thought which could be called "positivist" (being
exists, God exists by definition, if there has to be
some thing, it could only be this world and this
nature here, nothingness has no properties) and a
"negativist" thought (the first truth is that of a
doubt, what is certain first of all is a locus between
being and nothingness, the model of infinity is my
liberty, this world here is a pure fact) which inverts
the signs and perspectives of the former, without
either eliminating or coinciding with it? Do we not
find everywhere the double certitude that being exists, that appearances are only a manifestation and
a restriction of being—and that these appearances
are the canon of everything that we can understand

by "being," that in this respect it is being in-itself which appears as an ungraspable phantom, an *Unding*? Could we not find what has been called an "ontological diplopy" (Blondel), which after so much philosophical effort we cannot expect to bring to a rational reduction and which leaves us with the sole alternative of wholly embracing it, just as our gaze takes over monocular images to make a single vision out of them. Viewed in this way, the continual shifting of philosophies from one perspective to the other would not involve any contradiction, in the sense of inadvertence or incoherence, but would be justified and founded upon being. All one could do is to ask the philosopher to admit this phenomenon and to reflect upon it, rather than merely suffering it and occupying alternatively two ontological positions, each of which excludes and invites the other.

Perhaps then we would not regard the extraordinary confusion in modern ideas of nature, man, and God—the equivocations in "naturalism," "humanism," and "theism" (there is not one of these attitudes nowadays which does not slide into the other)—as nothing but decadence. If nowadays it happens that all the frontiers between these ideologies have broken down, this is because there is really, to borrow a phrase from Leibniz but in its strict sense, a "labyrinth of first philosophy." The task of philosophy should be to describe this labyrinth, to elaborate a concept of being such that its contradictions, neither accepted nor "transcended," still have their place. What was impossible for modern dialectical philosophies, because the dialectic which they contained remained bound by a predialectical ontology, would become possible in an ontology which reveals in being itself an overlap or movement.

We shall try here to arrive at this new ontology by following the recent development of the notion of nature. Applied science uncovers bodies of fact without ever achieving any radical self-expression, because it takes for granted traditional ontologies and never directly confronts the problem of being. But the transformations which it undergoes are full of philosophical significance. We shall attempt to develop these perspectives, to tie together the separate threads and to expose the "teleology" behind their progression.

We have gathered systematically last year's findings on the nature of physical being. At the very moment where twentieth-century physics has increased our power over nature to an unbelievable degree, it raises paradoxically the question of the meaning of its own truth in liberating itself from subjection to mechanical models and from figurative models in general. Physical action is no longer conceived as a trace in absolute space and time, passed on from one absolute individual to other equally absolute individuals. Physical entities, like mathematical entities, are no longer seen as "natures," but as "structures in an ensemble of operations." Determinism is no longer the tissue of the world: it is a crystallization on the surface of a "cloud" (Eddington). Some have remarked that this all reflects the return of "mentalism" in science. Others like Cassirer see in these developments a justification of critical idealism. On one point Cassirer is surely right: in the scientific description of the world there is no question of modern conceptions of causality implying an additional *factor* to be superimposed on the various determinisms. It is the latter which are always looked for, though what one discovers are only the supporting conditions outside of which the laws have no validity. What has occurred is a crisis in intuition rather than a crisis in science. For Cassirer, this crisis should make us understand once and for all what critical idealism had been teaching for a long time, namely, that symbolism does not have to be realized. Modern physics should disembarrass us not only of "materialism" and "mentalism," but of all philosophy of nature: nature is a "collection of relations which contain neither action nor passion." There can be no meaningful question concerning the *"Innere der Natur."* Nevertheless, this return to critical idealism does not take account of certain aspects of modern physics described by Cassirer himself. For there is a crisis, he says, not only of intuition, but of *Objektbegriff*. The field "is no longer a thing, it is a system of effects." But, if the concept of object is in dispute, how can critical idealism remain intact since it is entirely an analysis of the conditions and means of the positing of an object? Transcendental idealism loses its meaning if science has no power over the object.

What is called nature is certainly not a spirit at work in things whose aim is to resolve problems by "the most simple means"—but neither is it simply the projection of a power of thought or determination present in us. It is *that which makes there be,* simply, and at a single stroke such a coherent structure of a being, which we then laboriously express in speaking of a "space-time continuum," of "curved space," or simply of "the most determinate path" of the anaclastic line. Nature is that which establishes privileged states, the "dominant traits" (in the genetic sense of the word) which we try to comprehend through the combination of concepts—nature is an ontological derivation, a pure "passage," which is neither the only nor the best one possible, which stands at the horizon of our thought as a fact which there can be no question of deducing.

This facticity of nature is revealed to us in the universe of perception. Whatever the corrections which knowledge has to make in it, this universe regains an ontological signification that it had lost in classical science. As Niels Bohr has remarked, it is no accident that there is a harmony between the descriptions of psychology (we would say, of phenomenology) and the conceptions of contemporary physics. Moreover, the classical criticism of the perceived universe is bound to a mechanistic psychophysiology which can no longer be retained as such at a time when scientists are throwing doubt upon mechanistic metaphysics.

In the last half of the year we tried, in the same way, to specify the concept of organic nature implicit in contemporary science. The life sciences also never cease to introduce "operational" concepts whose obscurity should not be dissipated but circumscribed and reflected upon philosophically. There are, for example, the concepts of behavior (in the sense of Coghill and Gesell) and those of information and communication which, throughout all the discussion to which they give rise, elude the classical interpretations they were intended to rejoin. We attempted to analyze the notions of the possible, of totality, form, field, and signification around which these investigations gravitate.

Unlike that of physics, the development of the contemporary life-sciences does not occur in the form of extensive theoretical unifications. Thus instead of a connected account we can provide only samples and selections. Several lectures were devoted to the different levels of behavior.

Lower-order behavior was examined in terms of the perspective offered by J. von Uexüll and the notions of *Umwelt, Merkwelt* and *Wirkwelt* which he has introduced. We discussed the notion of *Subjektnatur* which he believed to be the conclusion of his findings. We traced the application of the concept of behavior in morphogenesis and physiology ("behavior in internal circuits," for example in E. S.

Russell).[1] This introduced the ideas of a thematization, in opposition to a "pushed-causality," and of a "directiveness," although limited and specialized and to that extent as different from the notion of entelechy as from the notion of machine. The forms of lower-order behavior also introduced us to a mutual cohesion between the parts of the organism, the organism and its surroundings, between organisms and the species, which involves a sort of presignification.

Reciprocally, we should find among the so-called higher levels of behavior (the study of which, by Lorenz for example, derives directly from Uexüll) something of the inertia of the body. If animal being is already a production (*faire*) then there is an activity of the animal which is not simply an extension of its being. In mimesis, where it is impossible to separate behavior and morphology, there appears a fundamental level of behavior where resemblance is operative, a "natural magic," or a vital undividedness, which involves neither finality nor a relation of understanding and representation. Portmann's idea of a reading of animal types (*Tiergestalt*), a study of their external appearance considered as an "organ for being seen," with its accompanying notion of an interanimality as necessary to the complete definition of the organism as its hormones and its "internal" processes, has offered further verifica-

---

1. E. S. Russell, *The Directiveness of Organic Activities* (Cambridge: At the University Press, 1945).—*Trans.*

tion of the theme of the organism's "form value." It is in terms of these notions that we opened up the study of "instinctive movements" of "sign stimuli," and of "innate activating schemas" referred to by Lorenz, trying to show that these do not imply any renewal of mechanism, suggested by the metaphors of lock and key, but of spontaneous styles of behavior which anticipate an aspect or element of the world and are occasionally sufficiently open to give rise to a fixation on a nonspecific element (*Prägung*). Thus, since the instinct is an oneiric or narcissistic preparation of external "objects," it is not surprising that it is capable of substitutions, displacements, of "action at a distance," and of "ritualizations" which do not merely superimpose themselves upon fundamental biological acts, such as copulation, but displace them, transfigure them, and submit them to conditions of "display" which reveal the appearance of a being who *sees* and *shows himself,* with the emergence of a symbolism whose "comparative philology" (Lorenz) [2] has yet to be constructed.

We also tried to get at the nature of vital being by following the method of epistemology, that is to say, through reflection upon the knowledge of living creatures. We inquired into the conditions under which we may validly attribute to a given animal one or more "senses," an associated milieu or "territory," a working relation with its cohort (Chauvin's

2. Konrad Lorenz, "Über tanzähnliche Bewegungsweisen bei Tieren," *Studium Generale*, V, no. 1 (1952).—*Trans.*

study of the migratory locust) and finally a symbolic life (Frisch's study of language in bees). It emerged that all zoology assumes from our side a methodical *Einfühlung* into animal behavior, with the participation of the animal in our perceptive life and the participation of our perceptive life in animality. In such phenomena we have found a new argument against the philosophical artificialism of neo-Darwinism in its most developed forms. The ultra-mechanism or ultra-finalism of the Darwinians rests upon the ontological principle of all or nothing: an organism *is* absolutely what it is; if it were not, it would have been deprived of existence by the given conditions. The result of this way of thinking is to mask the most remarkable characteristic of living homeostases, namely, invariance *through fluctuation*. Whether we are dealing with organisms or animal societies, we do not find things subject to a law of all or nothing, but rather dynamic, unstable equilibria in which every rearrangement resumes already latent activities and transfigures them by decentering them. As a result, one cannot conceive of the relations between species or between the species and man in terms of a hierarchy. What there is is a difference of quality and for this very reason living creatures are not superimposed upon one another, the transcendence of one by the other is, so to speak, lateral rather than frontal, and one meets all sorts of anticipations and reminiscences.

In order to make contact with indubitably organic facts, we came back to ontogenesis and to embryology in particular—and showed that mechanistic interpretations (Speeman) as well as those of Driesch lose what is essential in the new notion of the possible: namely, the possible conceived not as another eventual occurrence, but as an ingredient of the existing world itself, as *general reality.*

In terms of this preview, which we shall complete at the beginning of next year by sketching the problems of the systematic theory of descent, we may already say that the ontology of life, as well as that of "physical nature," can only escape its troubles by resorting, apart from all artificialism, to brute being as revealed to us in our perceptual contact with the world. It is only within the perceived world that we can understand that all corporeality is already symbolism. Next year we shall attempt to describe in more detail the emergence of symbolism in the transition to the level of the human body.[3]

3. "Symbolism and the Human Body"; see translator's note on p. 99.

10 / Philosophy as Interrogation[1]

WITH THE PERMISSION of the Minister of Education to abridge the course, we have decided to postpone until next year the continuation of the study we began on the ontology of nature,[2] and to devote this year to some general reflections on the meaning of this inquiry and the question of the possibility of philosophy today.

What exactly are we looking for when we try to abstract from nature the categories of substance, accident, potentiality, act, object, subject, in-itself, for-itself, which are traditionally involved in ontology? What can be the relation between the new

1. This course was announced as "Symbolism and the Human Body." We venture to redescribe it since, as is clear from the opening remarks, it is concerned with the question of the possibility of philosophy today.—*Trans.*

2. Permission to abridge the course was granted in order to give Merleau-Ponty more time to work on the manuscript of *The Visible and the Invisible.*—*Trans.*

ontology and classical metaphysics? Could it be the negation and the end of philosophy, or, on the contrary, is it perhaps the very same inquiry restored to its vital sources?

With Hegel something comes to an end. After Hegel, there is a philosophical void. This is not to say that there has been a lack of thinkers or of geniuses, but that Marx, Kierkegaard, and Nietzsche start from a denial of philosophy. We might say that with the latter we enter an age of non-philosophy. But perhaps such a destruction of philosophy constitutes its very realization. Perhaps it preserves the essence of philosophy, and it may be, as Husserl wrote,[3] that philosophy is reborn from its ashes.

We shall not find the answer to these questions by following the history of thought since Hegel. The great works to be found along this path are too preoccupied with the struggle against Hegel and classical metaphysics, and to this extent have too much in common with them, to permit us to see clearly what remains of philosophy in these non-philosophies. On this point their obscurities and equivocations are beyond repair. The interpretations which they offer, and which we believe enable us to ascertain their content, actually only reflect our own views and problems. Nowadays, any commentary

3. *Die Krisis der europäischen Wissenschaften und die transzendentale Phänomenologie,* ed. Walter Biemel, *Husserliana* VI (The Hague: Martinus Nijhoff, 1962) [English translation, *The Crisis of European Sciences and Transcendental Phenomenology,* by David Carr (Evanston, Ill.: Northwestern University Press, 1970)].

on Marx or even Nietzsche is actually only a disguised stand with regard to our own times. Through a turn of events which itself is legitimate, those writers who refused the title of philosophers and deliberately devoted themselves to deciphering their own times—even though they may provide a language for their successors, an interrogation, the beginnings of analyses with a quite new depth—cannot by contrast *guide* posterity: it is to posterity itself that they leave the task of giving the final meaning to their work. They live on in us rather than our having a clear perspective on them and we involve them in our own problems rather than solving theirs with ours.

Everything occurs as though these philosophers had anticipated a world which turns out to be our own, as though the world had made an effort to resemble what they had foretold. For once, thought was in advance of history, and the questions they raised illuminate the present in which we live. By contrast, their answers, the solutions which they offer to that history which they anticipated so well —whether it is Marx's praxis or Nietzsche's will to power—seem to us too simple. They were conceived in opposition to metaphysics yet within the shelter of the solid world of which metaphysics is a part. For us who have to deal with the bewitched world foreseen by Marx and Nietzsche their solutions are inadequate to the nature of the crisis. In place of a philosophy which—at least in principle and *ex officio*—stood for clarity against possibly different replies to the same problems, we see more and more a history of non-philosophy whose authors have as their sole common denominator a certain modern obscurity, a pure interrogation. We shall not find the new philosophy already developed in Marx or in Nietzsche. We have to create it, taking into account the world in which we live where it becomes clear that their negation of metaphysics cannot take the place of philosophy.

That is why, before examining two contemporary efforts, we wished to describe (without any pretense of being complete) some of the phenomena which, whether it be in the order of history or that of culture, discredit philosophy among us, perhaps eventually to bring it back to life.

With regard to the relations between men, even those thinkers who found no natural harmonies in this area did not, prior to our times, believe that society was condemned to chaos. Marx only described social relations as contradictory within the framework of a specific historical regime whose successor was marked out from the very start and his solution to the contradictions of history through history itself was universal, valid equally for nondeveloped as well as industrial societies. This core of universality around which history was to organize itself has disintegrated. It may properly be asked whether violence, the opacity of social relations and the difficulties of a world in which such questions are the order of the day and where such doubts are unavoidable (even to those in it who post up complete certitudes) secretes of itself a violence and a desperate counterviolence. History has exhausted the categories in which conservative thought confined it, and it has done the same with those of revolutionary thought. But it is not just that the human world is illegible, nature itself has become explosive. Technology and science range before us energies which are no longer *within* the framework of the world but are capable of destroying it. They provide us with means of exploration which, even before having been used, awaken the old desire and the old fear of meeting the absolute Other. What for centuries had, in the eyes of men, possessed the solidity of the earth now appears fragile; what was once our predestined horizon has now become a provisional perspective. But equally, since it is man who discovers and fabricates, a new prometheism is mixed with our experience of the prehuman world. An extreme naturalism and an extreme artificialism are inextricably associated, not only in the myths of everyday life, but also in the refined myths which arise, for example, out of the theory of information or neo-Darwinism.

Considering these facts alone, the balance of our experience would seem to be negative. But, in the order of culture and research, the relativization of what was believed to be the ground of history and of nature is already found to possess a new solidity. Whether one thinks of the rejection of a ready-made language, meaningful from the very start, which has occurred from Mallarmé to the surrealists, or of the rejection of "means of representation" and of the systems of equivalences constituted in modern painting, or, again, of the generalization of music beyond the traditional selections in tonal and instrumental music, the very understanding of the classical forms of art has been renewed by the transcendence of counterpoint systems and the search for nonfigurative invariants. In all these domains, as well as in psychoanalysis, considered as a social and almost popular phenomenon, disintegration has found a balance and is surpassed, in the case of the better practitioners, by a new sense of the plurality of possibilities; the menace of the technical spirit has been offset by the expectation of a free reintegration.

Among philosophers the positive aspect of experience is decidedly the dominant one. Driven to self-examination by the irrationalism of their times, as well as by the intrinsic evolution of their problems, philosophers have arrived at a definition of philosophy as the interrogation of its very own meaning and possibility. "What I seek under the name of philosophy," writes Husserl,[4] "as the goal and the field of my labor, I know naturally. And yet I do not know it. Has this 'knowledge' ever been sufficient for any true thinker (*Selbstdenker*)? Has "philosophy ever ceased to be a riddle to him in his life as a philosopher?"—But this problem, this astonishment before one's self, and the unhabituated and unhabit-

4. *Ibid.*, Appendix 28, Supplementary Text, pp. 508–13.

ual vision which is its result, are precisely philosophy, are "what, in the last analysis, *was intended* in
the hidden unity of intentional interiority, which
alone creates the unity of history." [5]

We have attempted to retrace the path by which
Husserl passed from "philosophy as a strict science"
to philosophy as pure interrogation—the same path
which led Heidegger to the negativist and anthropological themes to which the public reduced his early
writings, to a conception of Being which he no
longer calls philosophy—but which, as it has been
well remarked (J. Beaufret), is certainly not extra-
philosophical.

In Husserl it is clear that the pure interrogation
is not a residue from metaphysics, not its last breath
nor a yearning for its lost empire. It is the proper
means of opening us to the world, to time, to nature,
to contemporary and living history and a means of
accomplishing the perpetual ambitions of philosophy. For if anyone ever engaged in those ambitions,
it was indeed Husserl. He undertook them wholly
and naively at the beginning of the century when he
made philosophy an inventory of the "essences"
which, in every domain of experience, resist our
efforts at an imaginative variation and are thus the
invariants of the domain in question. But, even at
this time, he dealt with essences as they are experi-
enced by us, as they emerge from our intentional
life. This is what Husserl should have expressed, in

5. *Ibid.*, p. 74.

the middle period of his thought, in the doctrine of the "reduction" as a return to the immanent meaning of our experiences, and in the formula of "phenomenological idealism." However, the process of reduction needs to be scrutinized and clarified. It then appears to involve a paradox. In one sense, what it teaches us is already known to us in the natural attitude, through the "world thesis." But Husserl's analysis elucidates the bodily infrastructure of our relation with things and with others, and it appears difficult to "constitute" these brute materials out of the attitudes and operations of consciousness which derives from a different order, that of theoria and ideation. The method of reduction is jeopardized by this internal difficulty in the "constitutive phenomenology." It is similarly at issue through certain of its implications, which were at first unnoticed but caught Husserl's attention in the period of the *Cartesian Meditations* (1929) and when developed revealed the reduction as less of a method defined once and for all than the index of a multitude of problems. The philosopher who advocates the reduction speaks for everyone; he implies that what is evident for him is or could be for everyone; he therefore implies an intersubjective universe and remains, relative to that universe, in the attitude of naive faith. An integral philosophy ought to be able to explicate and to constitute that domain. But how can I give an account of my access to *the alter ego*—even if he were reduced to the "meaning" *alter*

ego—as the immanent operation of my consciousness? This would be tantamount to constituting the
other person as constituting, and, through him, to
reduce myself to the status of the one constituted.
Furthermore, with regard to what concerns the
other person, can I, or can he, with regard to what
concerns me, make the distinction which I make
between myself as the ultimate, constituting subject
and the empirical man in whom this constituting
subject is embodied—a distinction which I make
easily through reflection and by a secondary apper-
ception of which I am still the author? To an external observer, is not the ultimate and constituting
subject one and the same as existent with the empirical man? Is not Fichte's *Ichheit überhaupt* simply
Fichte? The *Cartesian Meditations* grasp both horns
of the dilemma: there is an indeclinable subjectivity, an insurmountable solipsism—and yet, for this
very subjectivity, there is an intentional "transgres-
sion" or "encroachment" which enables everything
which happens within itself to pass into the other
person.

   It is in the last work which Husserl himself
prepared for publication that the difficulties in the
phenomenological reduction make themselves felt
to the point where they broach upon a fresh mutation in the doctrine of the reduction. From then on
Husserl describes the reduction as an initial phase
of inquiry, characteristic of phenomenology—perhaps even coextensive with phenomenology. It is a

question here, he says, of a type of being which contains everything: *allumspannende Seinsweise* [6] —the return from an objective world to a *Leben-swelt* in whose continual flux are borne Nature and the objects of perception, as well as the constructions through which we grasp them with Cartesian exactness; it is the source in general of all the historical structures which help us to analyze or model our relations with others and with the truth. When translated in terms of the *Lebenswelt,* the antinomies in the constitution of *alter* or those in the world thesis cease to be hopeless. We no longer have to try to understand how a for-itself can think of another from the ground of its own absolute solitude or how it could think of a preconstituted world in the very moment that it constitutes the world: the inherence of the self-in-the-world or of the world-in-the-self, what Husserl calls the *Ineinander,* is silently inscribed in an all-embracing experience which composes these incompossibles, and philosophy becomes the enterprise of describing, outside of the logic and vocabulary at hand, the universe of living paradoxes. The reduction no longer involves a return to ideal being, but brings us back to the spirit of Heraclitus,[7] to an interweaving of horizons, to an open Being. Through having "forgotten" the flux of the natural and historical world, having reduced it to the constructions of the objectivity of the natural sciences, reason and philosophy have become incap-

6. *Ibid.,* p. 134.
7. *Ibid.,* p. 173.

able of understanding and so of mastering man's historical fate. The horizon of "infinite tasks" opened up in the sixteenth and seventeenth centuries has dropped out of sight, while reason and philosophy have compromised with an ideal of objectivism which made knowledge of the mind and history an impossibility.

Heidegger's path, no less than Husserl's, is difficult to trace, and for the same reasons—namely, that commentators have fixed upon what recalled for them philosophy's past. Hardly any have followed the authors in what was nevertheless their main effort: to recover through an absolutely new way of thinking the experience which underlies metaphysics. In the early works of Heidegger, the emphasis has been put upon the role of the concept of Nothingness and the definition of a man as the locus of Nothingness. That is why some have looked in Heidegger for the substitution of humanism in place of metaphysics, and, whether they have been happy to find metaphysics destroyed or have made use of it in order to restore it, they have misconstrued his views on the human situation as he described it. In both cases, commentators have missed what, from the Preface to *Sein und Zeit,* was the declared aim of his thought: not to describe existence, *Dasein* (which has been incorrectly translated in French as "human reality"), as a fundamental and autonomous sphere—but, through *Da-sein,* to get at Being, the analysis of certain human attitudes being undertaken only because man *is* the interrogation of Being. Soon after *Sein und Zeit,* the analysis of truth and our openness to truth took the all too well-known path of the descriptions of anxiety, freedom, and concern. Heidegger speaks less and less of the relation of *ekstasis* between us and being, which underlies the priority of the self and the centrifugal movement of the self toward being. He dissolves the equivocations by pointing out that for him there was never any question of reducing being to time, but of approaching being through time, that in an absolute sense Nothingness (the Nothing nihilates, the *nichtiges Nichts*) cannot be taken into consideration. Existence, in contrast to Beings, or the things that are there in the world, can, if one wishes, be treated as non-being, but that is not nothing or nihilation. It is beyond such correlatives—the object and the Nothing "nihilates"—that philosophy takes its start, namely, in a "there exists," in an "opening" toward "something," toward "that which is not nothing." It is this preobjective Being, between the inert essence or *quidditas* and the individual localized at a point of space-time, that is the proper theme of philosophy. It can be said of this Being—the rose, said Angelus Silesius, is "without any why," blooms because it blooms, the rose-spectacle, the rose-totality—that it has no cause outside of itself, and moreover is not the cause of itself, that it is without ground, being the absence in principle of any ground. What more can be said of this radiation of qualified being, of this active being, or action of "standing-in" as one translator has put it? Unlike other words, the word to be is not a sign to which one could find a corresponding "representation" or object: its meaning is not distinct from its operation, which is to make Being speak in us rather than us speak of Being. For how would we speak of Being, since those beings and shapes of Being, which open to us the only conceivable access to it, at the same time hide it from us by their mass, and since every unveiling is simultaneously a dissimulation? What has been called the "mystique" of Being —a word expressly rejected by Heidegger—is the effort to integrate truth with our capacity for error, to relate the incontestable presence of the world to its inexhaustible richness and consequent absence which it recuperates, to consider the evidence of Being in the light of an interrogation which is the only mode of expressing this eternal elusion. We have tried to show how a philosophy oriented in this way leads us to a complete reworking of the concepts ordinarily used in the analysis of language (such as those of sign, meaning, analogon, metaphor, symbol) and how it leads to the notion of an "ontological history" (*Seinsgeschichte*) which stands to an empirical history of human actions and passions as a philosophical apprehension of speaking stands to the analysis of linguistic materials.

If we call philosophy the quest of Being or the *Ineinander*, is not philosophy quickly brought to silence—that very silence which from time to time breaks into Heidegger's essays? But does not this come from Heidegger's search for a direct expression of what is fundamental at the very moment he is showing its impossibility? Is it not the result of his refusal of all the mirrors of Being? It is the aim of an inquiry such as we have pursued here on the ontology of nature to sustain through contact with existents and the exploration of the regions of Being the same attention to what is fundamental that remains the privilege and the task of philosophy.

11 / Husserl at the Limits of Phenomenology

SINCE WE STILL LACK a complete edition of Husserl's *Nachlass*, the following discussion can hardly pretend to be "objective" in the sense of saying just what was said or directly implied by Husserl in the whole context of his writings. But even when everything of Husserl is published, are we right to assume that the "objective" method would restore to us "the thought" of Husserl? Such an assumption would only be plausible if Husserl's thought, or that of any other philosopher, were simply a system of neatly defined concepts, arguments to perennial questions and replies in which problems are permanently solved. But what if the act of reflection changes the meaning of the concepts it employs and perhaps even the nature of its questions; what if its conclusions are merely the overall direction of a search which was transformed into a "work" by the ever premature interruption of a life's work? Then we could not define a philosopher's thought solely in terms of what he had achieved. We should have to take account of what until the very end he was struggling to bring to reflection. Naturally, this unfinished thought (*impensé*) must be shown to be present through the words which circumscribe and delimit it. But then these words must be understood through their lateral implications as much as through their manifest or frontal significance. We need what Husserl called a "poetry of the history of philosophy" that would give us access to an operant thought, which in the case of a contemporary thinker would not be so risky, and perhaps be the only mode of objectivity in treating one who has written: "*Das historisch an sich Erste ist unsere Gegenwart.*" [1]

While only a complete edition can validate our interpretation, although hardly ever dispense with it, why not start right now to study the texts? In view of the rumors and discussion which always arise around a posthumous doctrine, such a start is imperative. For there are some who fear or wish to see Husserl "deviate" into the path of irrationalism that they believe Heidegger took. The best approach to this problem is to study the texts, two of them in particular.

The first text to be considered is "Die Frage nach dem Ursprung der Geometrie als intentional-histo-

1. "Our present is intrinsically historical."—*Trans.*

risches Problem." [2] It is because ideality and historicity have a common source that it is not by chance
that there is an unfinished history of geometry
which remains open, while at the same time there is
a corpus of geometry which forms a system (*Total-
sinn*) in which the early steps seem to have been
cancelled insofar as they were partial or contingent
developments.

To discover that common source, one has only to
locate between the flow of events and the timeless
realm of meaning a third dimension, which would
be a subterranean history or the genesis of ideality.
Both the early stages of geometry as well as all its
later advances contain a certain surplus of meaning
over and beyond their manifest or literal sense as it
enters the experience of individual geometricians.
Each stage opens up a field and prepares themes
which their author can only see as an outline of
what is to come (*Urstiftung*), but which, when
handed down (*tradiert*) to succeeding generations
along with the earliest advances, become useful
through a sort of second creation (*Nachstiftung*).
In this process new dimensions of thought are
opened up until, once the development has run its
course and has ended up in a last re-creation (*End-
stiftung*), there intervenes a mutation in knowl-

2. *Die Krisis der europäischen Wissenschaften und die
transzendentale Phänomenologie*, ed. Walter Biemel, *Husserliana* VI (The Hague: Martinus Nijhoff, 1962), pp. 365–
86 [English translation, *The Crisis of European Sciences and
Transcendental Phenomenology*, by David Carr (Evanston,
Ill.: Northwestern University Press, 1970)].

edge, often the result of a return to the sources or the side-paths neglected by the mainstream, which results in a new interpretation of all that went before. The historical development or the *Beweglichkeit* of geometry only coincides with its ideal sense for the reason that the latter is the perception of a field, a beginning or an opening which requires an endless production and reproduction. The principal role of every idea, once it has been formulated, signed, and dated, is to make its literal repetition superfluous, to launch culture toward a future, to achieve oblivion, to be transcended, to outline the horizon of a geometry to come and to delimit a coherent domain. In turn, it is essential for any system of ideas to be born, and to yield to us only in the furrow of historicity. Even if we knew nothing about the originators of geometry, we would at least know that there had been such individuals; geometry is never a natural phenomenon like the stones and the mountains. It exists only in the "space of humanity"; it belongs to being which has become spiritual (*geistig geworden*) and will continue to do so. Spiritual being exists solely for a mind resolved to reflect actively, determined to go on, to plunge itself still further into the invisible realm of unreal creations. Ideality coincides with historicity because it rests upon acts and because "the only way to grasp an idea is to produce it." The idea is impalpable and invisible because it has been *made*. The historicity of an idea is not the fact of its inclusion in a series of events with a unique temporal location, or its origin in the mind of a particular man living at a certain place and time. It is its function to situate a task which is not uniquely its own, but one that echoes back to earlier beginnings. The historicity of an idea summons up the whole past and the entire future of culture as its witness. And to call upon so much history it has no need of documents, for history has its anchorage within itself, in the flesh of its sensible or natural existence, its active and productive being. It has only to reflect in order to know that thought makes itself, that it is culture and history.

How are we to understand this reverberation of the past and this pre-possession (*Vorhaben*) of the future of thought in any contemporary thought? In one sense geometry or any particular truth of geometry exists once for all, no matter how often it is thought of by individual geometricians. But if there was a pure and detached ideality, how would it enter the consciousness of he who discovers it, how would it come to birth in anyone's mind? Yet, on the other hand, if we start, as we must, from its birth in us, how shall we get from there to an ideal being, beyond any existing or possible mind? The only answer is that we do so by referring back to the implications of experience. A signification leaves its "place in consciousness" when it has been *said*. It is in virtue of being *Sinn von Reden* that it is there "for everyone," for every real or possible interlocutor. But language is "interwoven" (*verflochten*) with our horizon upon the world and humanity. Language is borne by our relation to the world and to others, which in turn supports and creates it. It is through language that our horizon is open and endless (*endlos*) and it is because we know that "everything has a name" that each thing exists and has a way of existing for us. To exist for us geometry inherits this linguistic tradition. But language only makes a signification universally available when it makes the objects of the world "public." Hence geometry is not merely an appropriation of a particular living mind, even though everyone agrees on such an ascription. Thus we have still not given a complete account of ideal being.

Neither have we exhausted the powers of "speech." Before anything else within my sphere of consciousness there is a sort of message from myself to myself: I can be sure today of thinking the same thought that I thought yesterday because the wake which it leaves is or could be retraced exactly by a fresh act of productive thought, which is the only veritable fulfillment of my recollected thought. I think in this near past, or rather yesterday's thought passes into today's thought: there is an encroachment of the passive upon the active which is reciprocal. Speech passes from the sphere of one consciousness to another by the same phenomenon of encroachment or propagation. As a speaking and active subject I encroach upon the other who is listening, as the understanding and passive subject I allow the other to encroach upon me. Within myself and in the exercise of language I experience activity in every case as the other side of passivity. And it is thus that ideality "makes its entrance" (*Eintritt*). No more in my relationship to myself than in my relationship to others is there any question of survey or of pure ideality. There is, however, the recuperation of a passivity by an activity: that is how I think within the other person and how I talk with myself. Speech is not a product of my active thought, standing in a secondary relation to it. It is my practice, my way of working, my *"Funktion,"* my destiny. Every production of the spirit is a response and an appeal, a coproduction.

But ideal being subsists outside of all actual communication, when the speaking subjects are asleep or are no longer living, and it seems to pre-exist speech, since there are men yet to be born who later will form valid ideas and these ideas are no less valid at this present moment. However, this does not place ideal being outside of speech, but merely obliges us to introduce an essential mutation in speech, namely, the appearance of writing. It is writing which once and for all translates the meaning of spoken words into ideal being, at the same time transforming human sociability, inasmuch as writing is "virtual" communication, the speaking of x to x, which is not carried by any living subject and belongs in principle to everyone, evoking a total speech. But the pure meaning contained in the written page which sublimates the solidity of things and then communicates that sublimation to thought is also a petrified meaning, sedimented, latent or dormant, insofar as no living spirit comes along to arouse it. The moment one touches the total meaning, one touches upon absence and the forgotten as well. Living meaning extends far beyond our explicit thoughts, but it is only open and without an end; it is not infinite. The sedimentation which makes it possible for us to go further is also responsible for us being threatened by hollow thoughts and for the sense of origins becoming void. The true cannot be defined outside of the possibility of the false.

We have now reached Husserl's last meditations on my relation to myself and to others, of which we can get a glance, while waiting for the publication of the manuscripts, from a fine study by Eugen Fink.[3] Passivity and activity, the spontaneous "I" and sensible time, cannot remain mutually external since I function as thinker identical through time and intersubjectivity is also in play. There is thus a sort of "simultaneity" of the one and the other, an *Urgegenwart* which has no locus between the before and after, an *Ur-Ich* anterior to the plurality of monads which cannot be said to be singular either, because it precedes both unity and plurality—true "negativity," "diremption," a being prior to the distinction between essence and existence. These words, says Fink, project the new dimension of *Le-*

3. "Die Spätphilosophie Husserls in der Freiburger Zeit," in *Edmund Husserl, 1859–1959, Phaenomenologica* IV (The Hague: Martinus Nijhoff, 1960), pp. 99–115.

benstiefe which opens up in the writings of Husserl's later period. But for Husserl this speculative vocabulary was only an aid to description, a means of outlining the operation of the transcendental life which he always sought to catch in the act, analytically. His philosophy is not congealed in "results," or "points of view." Moreover, Husserl's later philosophy is no finished product, no fixed possession of the cultural spirit, no house in which one can dwell comfortably. "Everything is open, all its paths lead out into the open." [4] To come back to the problem of ideality, Husserl's analyses foreshadow Heidegger's thoughts on the way speech speaks.[5]

The notions of openness and horizon, employed in the fragment on the origin of geometry with regard to superstructures and ideal being, are to be found also with regard to the "base" in a text from 1934, *Umsturz der kopernikanischen Lehre*.[6] For the Copernican, the world contains only "bodies" (*Körper*). Through meditation we must again learn of a mode of being whose conception we have lost, the being of the "ground" (*Boden*), and that of the earth first of all—the earth where we live, that which is this side of rest and movement, being the ground from which all rest and all movement are

4. *Ibid.*, pp. 113–14.
5. *Unterwegs zur Sprache* (Pfullingen: Neske, 1958), pp. 12–13.
6. Unpublished. We have this from communication in 1939 with Professor Aron Gurwitsch, one of Husserl's students.

separated, which is not made out of *Körper*, being the "source" from which they are drawn through division, which has no "place," being that which surrounds all place, which lifts all particular beings out of nothingness, as Noah's Ark preserved the living creatures from the Flood. There is a kinship between the being of the earth and that of my body (*Leib*) which it would not be exact for me to speak of as moving since my body is always at the same distance from me. This kinship extends to others, who appear to me as other bodies, to animals whom I understand as variants of my embodiment, and finally even to terrestrial bodies since I introduce them into the society of living bodies when saying, for example, that a stone "flies." To the degree that I adopt the Copernican constitution of the world, I abandon my own standpoint, I pretend to be an absolute observer, forgetting my terrestrial roots which nevertheless nourish everything else, and I come to consider the world as the pure object of an infinite reflection before which there are only objects conformable to itself. But such an idealization cannot provide its own foundation, and the sciences of the infinite are experiencing a crisis. The type of being which our experience of the earth and the body reveals to us is no curiosity of external perception but has a philosophical signification. Our implantation envelops a view of space and temporality, a view of natural causation, of our "territory." It envelops an *Urhistorie* which binds all existing or possible societies insofar as they all inhabit the same "earthly" space, in the broadest sense, and finally it contains a philosophy of the world as *Offenheit der Umwelt,* in opposition to the "represented" infinite of the classical sciences of nature.

12 / Nature and Logos: The Human Body

First of all, we have completed our analysis from earlier years of certain examples of biological thought relative to the organic development of the organism, and the problems of ontogenesis and phylogenesis. It seemed to be of interest to follow the detours in Driesch's thinking inasmuch as contemporary embryology is still preoccupied with the same questions raised by Driesch over sixty years ago. Driesch maintained that the organism cannot be reduced to its state at any given moment, since the activities of regulation and regeneration are indications of an excess of the potential over the actual. At the same time, Driesch was reluctant to label these potentialities "prospective powers," since it would be necessary to add a principle of order which guaranteed the invariance of the type, and since in combination these two principles would obviously only be an "analytic" expression of what took place. Occasionally, however, Driesch regards development as a network of reciprocal actions in which the "directive stimuli" interact with one another, which would leave the factor E (entelechy) with nothing more than a symbolic value. Nevertheless, Driesch is not free from the alternatives of the machine or life: if the organism is not a machine, then entelechy must be "the expression of a true reality, of a veritable element of nature," and since this reality is invisible to science, there must be a "thought" or philosophy which takes the place of science to determine this second positivity indirectly designated by science. Here what is instructive is that, while making the transition to "philosophy," Driesch, who is an exacting thinker, feels constrained to deny entelechy the status of energy, transformer of energy, or even "releaser," recognizing in it only the power to suspend suspensions or equilibria, and finally delimiting it as simply "a complicated system of negations." [1] One could only go further, he says, by departing from the experience of "my body" and its relation with space—a path familiar to our contemporaries, but which only leads back to the same problems if "my body" is only an island in a mechanical world. In our opinion, the difficulties which Driesch encountered show that life is incomprehensible both to the philosophy of the object (mechanism *and* vitalism) and to the philosophy of the idea, and can only be clarified

1. A. E. Driesch, *The Science and Philosophy of the Organism* (London: A. and C. Black, 1929).—*Trans.*

through a philosophy of "something," or, as one says nowadays, a philosophy of structure. Embryology since Driesch seems to us to have been moving in this direction in refusing to opt either for preformation or epigenesis, rather taking both notions as "complementary" and describing embryogenesis as a "flux of determination." The appearance of the notions of "gradient" and "fields"—that is to say, of "organo-formative" territories which impinge upon one another and possess a periphery beyond their focal region in which regulation is only probable—represents a mutation in biological thought as important as anything in physics. Physicists are rejecting both the restriction of space and the resort to a second positive causality; they conceive life as a sort of reinvestment of physical space, the emergence of original macrophenomena between the microphenomena, "singular areas" of space or "enveloped phenomena."

The need for new theoretical frameworks is also felt in the study of phylogenesis. The neo-Darwinists had attempted to frame their descriptions of the "style" or "design" of evolution (micro-evolution, macro-evolution, mega-evolution) in the schema of selection-mutation inherited from Darwin. But they managed to do so only by weighting their schema with a quite new sense, so that in a recent work Simpson writes: "The cause of an evolutionary event is the *total* situation preceding it . . . so that it is not entirely realistic to attempt designation of separate causal elements within that situation. At most, one may speak of 'factor complexes' or 'constellations.' " [2] From this point of view, there is no longer any place for argument over the predominance of mutation or selection in evolution taken as a whole, and that should (though it hardly will) put an end to the endless debate over the internal and external direction of evolutionary trends. These apparent alternatives are lacking in reality; put in these terms they carry no weight: in truth, they are meaningless.

In opposition to the Darwinian tradition, "idealist morphology" has little trouble in showing that relations of descent are far from being the only ones to deserve consideration. Speculation upon the genetic series even raises questions in the philosophy of history (essential and accidental relations—the primitive and the simple—problem of stages) and cannot be treated as a summary of facts from zoological generation or descendence (Dacqué [3]). But "idealist morphology" restricts itself to vindicating its descriptive powers against the claims of mechanism. It situates the ideas which it introduces in *our* thought, and, in keeping with the Kantian tradition, reserves the interior of nature to an inaccessible reality. A truly statistical conception of evolution would, on the contrary, attempt to define vital being starting from phenomena; it would impose the prin-

2. G. G. Simpson, *The Major Features of Evolution* (New York: Columbia University Press, 1953), p. 59.
3. E. Dacqué, *Organische Morphologie und Pälaontologie* (Berlin: Borntraeger, 1935).—*Trans.*

ciples of an "evolutionary kinetic" free from any schema of timeless causality or constraint from microphenomena, and would openly admit a scalar structure of reality, a plurality of "space-time levels." Organisms and types would then appear as "traps for fluctuations," as "patterned jumbles," as variants of a sort of "phenomenal topology" (F. Meyer), without any break with chemical, thermodynamic and cybernetic causation.

Our purpose was to get to the appearance in nature of man and the human body. If the development of life is a "phenomenon," that is to say, if it is reconstructed by us on the basis of our own life, then it cannot be derived as an effect from a cause. Furthermore (and this is the difference between phenomenology and idealism), life is not a simple *object* for a *consciousness*. In previous courses we have shown that life and external nature are unthinkable without reference to perceived nature. Now we must think of the human body (and not "consciousness") as that which perceives nature which it also inhabits. Thus the relation between *Ineinander* which we thought we perceived can be recovered and confirmed. The object of the last part of the course was to describe the animation of the human body, not in terms of the descent into it of pure consciousness or reflection, but as a metamorphosis of life, and the body as the "body *of* the spirit" (Valéry).

The latter purpose would demand an "esthesiology," a study of the body as a perceiving animal. For there can be no question of analyzing the fact of birth as if a body-instrument had received from elsewhere a thought-pilot, or inversely as if an object called the body had mysteriously produced consciousness out of itself. We are not dealing here with two natures, one subordinate to the other, but with a double nature. The themes of the *Umwelt,* of the body schema, of perception as true mobility (*Sichbewegen*), popularized in psychology and nerve physiology, all express the idea of corporeality as an entity with two faces or two "sides." Thus the body proper is a sensible and it is the "sensing"; it can be seen and it can see itself; it can be touched and it can touch itself, and, in this latter respect, it comprises an aspect inaccessible to others, open in principle only to itself. The body proper embraces a philosophy of the flesh as the visibility of the invisible.

If I am capable of feeling by a sort of interlocking of the body proper and the sensible, I am capable also of seeing and recognizing other bodies and other men. The schema of the body proper, since I am able to see myself, can be shared by all other bodies, which I can also see. The body schema is a lexicon of corporeality in general, a system of equivalences between the inside and the outside which prescribes from one to the other its fulfillment in the other. The body which possesses senses is also a body which has desires and thus esthesiology expands into a theory of the libidinal body. The theoretical concepts of Freudianism are corrected and affirmed once they are understood, as suggested in the work of Melanie Klein, in terms of corporeality taken as itself the search of the external in the internal and of the internal in the external, that is, as a global and universal power of incorporation. The Freudian libido is not an entelechy of sex, nor is sex a unique and total cause but rather an ineluctable dimension outside of which nothing human can abide since nothing which is human is entirely incorporeal. A philosophy of the flesh finds itself in opposition to any interpretation of the unconscious in terms of "unconscious representations," a tribute paid by Freud to the psychology of his day. The unconscious is feeling itself, since feeling is not the intellectual possession of "what" is felt, but a dispossession of ourselves in favor of it, an opening toward that which we do not have to think in order that we may recognize it. Is the notion of an unconscious state adequate to the facts of repression, the mode of existence of the "primitive scene" and its power of seduction and fascination? The double formula of the unconscious ("I did not know" and "I have not always known it") corresponds to two aspects of the flesh, its poetic and its oneiric powers. When Freud presents the concept of repression in all its operational richness, it comprises a double movement of progress and regression, of openness toward the adult universe and of a relapse to the pregenital life, but henceforth called by its name, having become unconscious "homosexuality" (*From the History of an Infantile Neurosis*).[4] Thus the repressed unconsciousness would be a secondary formation, contemporary with the formation of a system of perception—consciousness—and the primordial unconsciousness would be a permissive being, the initial yes, the undividedness of feeling.

The preceding leads to the idea of the human body as a natural symbolism; an idea, rather than being final, announced, on the contrary, a sequel. We may ask what could be the relation between this tacit symbolism, or undividedness, and the artificial or conventional symbolism, which seems to be privileged, to open us toward ideal being and to truth. The relation between the explicit logos of the sensible world will form the topic of another series of courses.

4. *The Complete Works of Sigmund Freud,* vol. XVII (London: Hogarth Press, 1955).—*Trans.*